London
through a lens

timeout.com

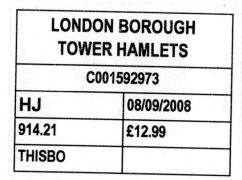

LONDON BOROUGH TOWER HAMLETS	
C001592973	
HJ	08/09/2008
914.21	£12.99
THISBO	

Published by Time Out Guides Ltd, a wholly owned subsidiary of Time Out Group Ltd.
Time Out and the Time Out logo are trademarks of Time Out Group Ltd.

© Time Out Group Ltd 2008

10 9 8 7 6 5 4 3 2 1

This edition first published in Great Britain in 2008 by Ebury Publishing
A Random House Group Company
20 Vauxhall Bridge Road, London SW1V 2SA

Random House Australia Pty Limited 20 Alfred Street, Milsons Point, Sydney, New South Wales 2061, Australia
Random House New Zealand Limited 18 Poland Road, Glenfield, Auckland 10, New Zealand
Random House South Africa (Pty) Limited Isle of Houghton, Corner Boundary Road & Carse O'Gowrie, Houghton 2198, South Africa

Random House UK Limited Reg. No. 954009

Distributed in USA by Publishers Group West
1700 Fourth Street, Berkeley, California 94710

Distributed in Canada by Publishers Group Canada
250A Carlton Street, Toronto, Ontario M5A 2L1

For further distribution details, see www.timeout.com

ISBN: 978-1-84670-110-8

A CIP catalogue record for this book is available from the British Library

Printed and bound in Singapore by Tien Wah Press Ltd

The Random House Group Limited supports The Forest Stewardship Council (FSC), the leading international forest certification organisation. All our titles that are printed on Greenpeace approved FSC certified paper carry the FSC logo. Our paper procurement policy can be found at www.rbooks.co.uk/environment

Time Out carbon-offsets all its flights with Trees for Cities (www.treesforcities.org).

Time Out Guides Limited
Universal House
251 Tottenham Court Road
London W1T 7AB
Tel + 44 (0)20 7813 3000
Fax + 44 (0)20 7813 6001
Email guides@timeout.com
www.timeout.com

Editorial
Editor Cath Phillips
Proofreader John Pym
Indexer Jonathan Cox

Managing Director Peter Fiennes
Financial Director Gareth Garner
Editorial Director Sarah Guy
Series Editor Cath Phillips
Editorial Manager Holly Pick
Assistant Management Accountant
Ija Krasnikova

Design
Art Director Scott Moore
Art Editor Pinelope Kourmouzoglou
Senior Designer Henry Elphick
Graphic Designer Gemma Doyle, Kei Ishimaru
Digital Imaging Simon Foster
Ad Designer Jodi Sher

Picture Desk
Picture Editor Jael Marschner
Deputy Picture Editor Katie Morris
Picture Researcher Gemma Walters

Advertising
Commercial Director Mark Phillips
Sales Manager Alison Wallen
Advertising Assistant Kate Staddon

Marketing
Head of Marketing Catherine Demajo
Marketing Manager Yvonne Poon
Sales & Marketing Director North America Lisa Levinson

Production
Group Production Director Mark Lamond
Production Manager Brendan McKeown
Production Controller Caroline Bradford
Production Coordinator Julie Pallot

Time Out Group
Chairman Tony Elliott
Financial Director Richard Waterlow
Group General Manager/Director Nichola Coulthard
Time Out Magazine Ltd MD Richard Waterlow
TO Communications Ltd MD David Pepper
Managing Director, Time Out International
Cathy Runciman
Group IT Director Simon Chappell

Contributors Jessica Cargill Thompson, Nick Royle, Sarah Thorowgood, Yolanda Zappaterra.

The Editor would like to thank Matthew Butson and Caroline Theakstone at Getty Images, Sarah Guy, Pete Watts.

Photography Getty Images (www.gettyimages.com).

Contents

Introduction

This isn't a guidebook, or a history book, or a chronological survey of photography in London. Yes, some tourist hotspots and iconic buildings do appear, from Trafalgar Square and St Paul's Cathedral to the Crystal Palace and Tate Modern. And, yes, the period covered ranges from almost the birth of photography – William Henry Fox Talbot's faded calotype of Nelson's Column under construction, taken in 1843 – to the 21st century. But, as you'll see, *London through a lens* (inspired by *Time Out* magazine's slot of the same name) isn't arranged by date or district or theme. Just as the capital is a jumbled conglomeration that has grown messily over the centuries, the layout of its streets tortured and chaotic, its layers of history crashing into one another like tectonic plates rather than forming a neatly arranged sandwich, so this book mixes images of Victorian streets with 1930s racing cars and modern-day skateboarders. Carefully composed portraits sit alongside casual snapshots; front-page news photos appear next to pictorialist prints.

Although the images come from one library – the vast archives of Getty Images – they're also drawn from many sources: the myriad collections that make up those archives. So there are photographs from Fleet Street newspapers (*Evening Standard*, *Daily Express*) and from magazines (in particular, *Picture Post*, that ground-breaking purveyor of 20th-century photojournalism), from one of the earliest commercial photography agencies (the London Stereoscopic Company, founded in 1854) and from books of social documentary (John Thomson's pioneering case studies of London street life in the 1870s).

There are a few well-known images in here: the Sex Pistols bursting out of a studio doorway, for instance, in a cloud of beery froth, having just shocked the nation by swearing on live TV. An image that made the front page of the *Daily Mirror* and somehow enscapsulated the impact punk had on late 1970s Britain. And some landmark events too: the Jarrow Crusade; the Battle of Cable Street; the 1968 protest in Grovesnor Square against the Vietnam war; the Festival of Britain; Chamberlain on his return from Munich clutching the piece of paper that he hoped, forlornly it turned out, would avert a world war. And some famous names crop up, both in front of and behind the lens. The Beatles, Emmeline Pankhurst, Michael Caine and Gandhi all take a bow, as do some of Britain's most acclaimed photographers, including Bill Brandt and Robert Howlett, Thurston Hopkins and Terry Fincher.

But if the momentous has its place, so does the mundane. The great and the good (and the not so good) are outnumbered by everyday people doing everyday things. You'll find plenty of images of daily life, showing nameless Londoners on unnamed streets: an Italian ice-cream seller in Putney on a hot summer's day; a huge crowd of football fans in open stands at Highbury; two skaters practising their moves on a frozen pond in Wimbledon. And in most cases the people who took the photographs are as anonymous as the people featured in them. We've included some pictures because they're amusing or just plain bizarre: why, exactly, did that helmeted chap fly a tiny wingless stunt plane down a steep ramp at Alexandra Palace one fine day in 1930? We don't know, but we're glad somebody bothered to record the event for posterity.

We hope, also, that this book captures something of the ephemeral and the everlasting nature of this great metropolis; that it shows how much London has changed, and how much it hasn't. The four chimneys of Battersea Power Station have formed an iconic profile on the skyline for so long that it's hard to believe that for 20 years Londoners gazed up at just two towers. Similarly, the gothic turrets of Tower Bridge are now such a tourist cliché that seeing the structure as a half-finished skeleton comes as a shock. Some images manage to be both surprising and familiar. Buskers may have been a common sight on the streets for as long as there have been streets – but performing bears? That does seem to come from another world, though the people, the houses, everything else in the picture (an early example of candid street photography by Paul Martin) could have been taken yesterday. Look at the grinning faces of the grubby urchins scrabbling for coal during the General Strike of 1926 and the similarity with today's children is probably more striking (despite the poverty) than the differences.

The result is, of course, in no way exhaustive or comprehensive. The selection of pictures chosen is but a tiny sampling of what's hidden in the endless boxes and filing cabinets in Getty Images' warehouses, and the subjects depicted are a mere fraction of what London has (and had) to offer. Think of it as an idiosyncratic photo album, amassed by a very long-lived relative with wide-ranging tastes (and a somewhat odd sense of humour). Put simply, we chose these pictures because we liked them. We hope you like them too.

Cath Phillips, Editor

A history in pictures

Matthew Butson, vice president of Hulton I Archive, charts the development of the world's largest image collection.

Within two unprepossessing warehouses in a west London side street sits one of the greatest and oldest photographic archives on the planet, containing myriad collections that run from the birth of photography to the present day. Visitors are often left dumbfounded by the sheer size and scale of the library. Officially the Hulton I Archive, but more usually known as just the Hulton, it is one of the hidden jewels of London, housing a great chunk of Britain's visual heritage. Though not a museum in the strict sense of the word, the Hulton is as much a cultural resource as it is a commercial business. An ongoing programme of conservation and preservation maintains the archive and ensures that future generations can continue to be inspired by the medium of photography. It also features an impressive array of engravings, etchings, lithographs, antiquarian maps, cartoons, woodcuts, illustrations and related visual ephemera, drawing from almost the beginning of printed media and the invention of the Caxton press.

In the beginning

The Hulton can trace its roots back 150 years to the founding of the London Stereoscopic Company in 1854. Based in London and counting such early photography luminaries as William England and Reinhold Thiele among its ranks, LSC was one of the world's first photographic businesses to license its imagery for commercial purposes. It also made photographic plates and cameras. In addition to general scenic views, LSC produced everything from studio portraits to a 'comic series' of humorous stereographs (an early form of 3D photography), including an extensive array of pictures taken in the capital between the 1850s and 1910s – now probably the most comprehensive collection of 19th-century photographs of London in existence.

The LSC thrived for more than 60 years, but found it could not compete with the early 20th-century invention of half-tone reproduction in newspapers. Very soon, anyone with a ha'penny to spare could gaze upon photos from around the world, a pastime until then reserved for the privileged few. In 1910, the firm closed its offices in Oxford Street, Regent Street and Cheapside. After some years in storage – with the glass negatives narrowly escaping being turned into greenhouses shortly after World War I – the collection was acquired by the Rischgitz Studios in 1922, which, in turn, was acquired by Hulton Press in 1947.

The birth of Picture Post

A decade earlier, in 1937, British publishing magnate Edward Hulton had appointed the Hungarian Jewish émigré Stefan Lorant (then editor of the successful pocket journal *Lilliput*) to create a national weekly to add to Hulton's growing stable of titles – and the seminal photojournalism magazine *Picture Post* was born. A publishing phenomenon from the outset, *Picture Post* outstripped its original print run with a first-issue circulation of over one million. The magazine's liberal, anti-fascist, populist stance, coupled with candid 35mm pictures by a slew of extraordinarily talented photographers, made it a runaway success. During the war years, *Picture Post* was required reading in Britain – at times its 'readership' was reported to be over 80 per cent of the population.

Picture Post's approach was similar to the US magazine *Life*, which had itself taken a lead from Lorant's pioneering magazine work in Germany in the 1920s. Using the picture essay format, Lorant commissioned articles and photographs on a wide range of subjects by the leading European photojournalists of the day. Between 1938 and 1957, over 9,000 articles were commissioned for *Picture Post*; only 2,000 were actually used (not that uncommon a percentage for a magazine of its kind at the time) and the other 7,000 were filed away. Since fewer than a dozen photographs usually accompanied each article and the photographers regularly delivered hundreds of negatives, a colossal archive of unpublished, often unprinted, images built up, which today offers a mouth-watering reservoir of untapped history.

Lorant's role at *Picture Post* didn't last long. In 1940, he emigrated to the States; having been imprisoned in Germany during the rise of Nazism, he was fearful of what would happen if Hitler invaded Britain. He didn't return for many decades. Meanwhile, the magazine thrived into the 1950s under the editorship of the left-leaning Tom Hopkinson, a protégé of Lorant.

Famous photographers such as Kurt Hutton, Felix Man and Bert Hardy and journalists of the stature of Fyfe Robertson, Macdonald Hastings, Trevor Philpot and James Cameron were sent out with no further brief than to come back with a good story. Bert Hardy – every inch a Cockney with an innate gift for connecting with people from all walks of life, as well as the ability to capture the 'decisive moment' – perhaps epitomises why *Picture Post* was such a huge success, and the body of work he left behind still inspires today.

Since the weekly was based in London, many essays focused on the capital, covering every aspect of life, warts and all – from children playing street games in the East End to the pomp and circumstance of Queen Elizabeth II's coronation. In 1950, Hardy and Cameron sent back a sensational piece about the execution of South Koreans by their fellow countrymen while under the guard of British and US troops. With his knighthood pending, Hulton refused to run a story that he felt was scurrilous and over-critical of the United Nations and sacked Hopkinson. The magazine limped on under a succession of picture editors until it folded in 1957; the advent of commercial television and the loss of advertising revenue were partly to blame, but it was felt that *Picture Post* was never quite the same after Hopkinson and had lost its edge.

Other acquisitions

The Hulton Picture Post Library didn't just contain the thousands of photos commissioned for *Picture Post*. Edward Hulton became increasingly interested in the growing archive and began actively acquiring new material. Collection after collection was added, including the London Stereoscopic Company's archives; Augustin Rischgitz's collection of prints, engravings and early photos; the renowned Hungarian agent Henry Guttmann's valuable holdings of European imagery; and the Sasha (Alex Stewart) Collection of outstanding British studio and theatre photography, much of it shot in the West End. Towards the end of the World War II, the problem of how properly to catalogue the huge bank of images became acute. So, in 1945, Hulton commissioned Charles Gibbs-Smith of the Victoria & Albert Museum to create the world's first indexing system for pictures. The Gibbs-Smith system was later adopted by the V&A, parts of the British Museum's collection and is still in operation at Hulton today.

The BBC and beyond

Following the demise of *Picture Post*, Edward Hulton sold his photo library to the BBC. The corporation was mainly interested in using the archive for its own in-house needs, and to a degree the collections stagnated. There were some additions, most notably of the Topical Press Agency – a Fleet Street-based operation founded in 1907 whose coverage of events in the capital (especially news, politics and sport) is particularly impressive.

In 1983, the collections of the *Daily Express* and *Evening Standard* newspapers were acquired, saving them from almost certain oblivion. Along with a number of national and regional newspapers in the 1970s and '80s, the *Express* and *Standard* saw little value in their image archives, and it was only a chance family connection between the Express newspaper group and the Hulton Library that meant they were preserved (many collections have been rescued from obscurity or destruction during Hulton's long history). More material from the two newspapers was added in 1985 and 1990. London has always been the epicentre of the media world in Britain, so it's not surprising that the vast majority of photographic agencies were based in the capital, which is why such a large percentage of Hulton I Archive's UK press and feature collections have a London bias.

At the end of the 1980s, after three decades of ownership, the BBC sold the picture archive into private hands. The new owner, a cable TV entrepreneur, quickly doubled the size of the library by acquiring the Keystone archives. Made up of three major Fleet Street press collections and a New York agency, this amounted to nearly eight million images. Most important from a London perspective, Keystone included the famed Fox Photos collection. In business from 1924 to 1984, Fox specialised in pictures of ordinary people doing ordinary things and, through the genius of street photographers such as Reggie Speller, Harry Todd and Binnie Hales, managed to capture the life and times of the capital every which way.

The library also moved home, from four different sites into its current location in west London, bringing millions of images together under one roof for the first time. Specialist staff started to hunt through and identify the earliest and rarest images. The process was akin to an archaeological dig, uncovering calotypes, daguerreotypes and carbon and vintage prints by 19th-century greats such as Julia Margaret Cameron, Lewis Carroll and Eadweard Muybridge, as well as work by 20th-century masters such as Brassai, Henri Cartier-Bresson and Man Ray. More than 30,000 prints were set aside in the purpose-built Vintage Room.

This includes a wealth of London material, from John Thomson and Paul Martin's pioneering street photography at the end of the 19th century to Bill Brandt's 'Doomed East End' from the 1930s. There's also a sequence showing the construction of the 1851 Great Exhibition in Sydenham, a series of 19th-century albumen panoramas of the Thames by Victor Prout, and 47 hand-coloured panels depicting the Duke of Wellington's funeral procession in 1852. What's fascinating about much of this material is that it shows familiar London sights in unfamiliar ways, unimpeded by later buildings – from St Paul's Cathedral to various royal palaces and the Pool of London before Canary Wharf – as well as theatres, railway stations, markets and other once-famous landmarks that disappeared long ago.

In 1996 the Hulton Collection was sold to the Getty Communications Group (now Getty Images), followed swiftly by the launch of a website and the Getty Images Gallery near Oxford Circus. The Hulton is unique within the world of commercial photography not only to run a traditional black and white darkroom, but also to employ a curator and conservator (both full-time) to look after the vast collection. Effectively, it's a living photo museum housed in a temperature- and humidity-controlled environment with a rolling programme of museum-standard conservation projects to preserve the overall collection for future.

Into the 21st century

In 2001, Getty Images merged the Hulton holdings with Archive Film & Photos (originally based in New York and born out of Pictorial Parade, one of the oldest continuously operated photo syndication agencies in the States) to create the Hulton | Archive of more than 50 million images contained within 1,500 individual collections. Since then, the addition of other archives from home and abroad, plus partnerships with British agencies such as Popperfoto that also have extensive London material, have resulted in the largest collection of images under one roof in the world – currently 70 million images and counting. Given that less than one per cent of the Hulton | Archive is currently accessible online and the cataloguing process is ongoing, there are still treasures to be unearthed and significant new finds are commonplace, be it a valuable orginal print or simpy a stunning image that has been 'lost' for years. The Hulton continues to evolve, much like London itself, and both are the envy of the world.

Nelson's Column 1843

One of the earliest photos of London, taken by William Henry Fox Talbot, who revolutionised photography by creating the calotype. The resulting image lacked the hard-edge clarity of its rival, the daguerreotype (invented by Frenchman Louis Daguerre), but it created a negative, allowing for limitless positive prints to be made – unlike the one-off daguerreotype. Nelson's Column was unveiled shortly after this picture was taken (from a window in Cockspur Street), almost 40 years after a monument to the naval hero was suggested, following his death at the Battle of Trafalgar in 1805. The design competition was won by William Railton's granite Corinthian column, topped by a 17-foot high statue by EH Bailey of the one-armed admiral.

William Henry Fox Talbot/Hulton Archive

Nelson's Column 1900

Taken almost 60 years later than Fox Talbot's photograph, from almost exactly the same position. The fountains were added a couple of years after the column was finished, though these aren't the current version: they were remodelled in 1939 by Sir Edwin Lutyens and the bronze mermaids, mermen and dolphins added after World War II. Sir Edwin Landseer's four bronze lions arrived in 1867, while the plinth in the south-east corner of the square (empty in Fox Talbot's picture) is now occupied by a statue of Sir Henry Havelock, erected posthumously in 1861 to commemorate the major general's endeavours during the Indian Mutiny of 1857. The 'knifeboard' bus in the foreground – with back-to-back seating on the roof – was first introduced in 1851 to cope with the influx of tourists for the Great Exhibition.

London Stereoscopic Company/Hulton Archive

Painting the Penguin Pool 1936

Decorators are ignored by resident king penguins who waddle about their business as their home is given a lick of paint. London Zoo's Penguin Pool was designed in 1934 by modernist architect Berthold Lubetkin, a Russian émigré and co-founder of the radical Tecton group. He used reinforced concrete to create a sculptural form, the pool's elliptical shape and interlocking spiral ramps giving it a dynamic feel. In 2005 the penguins were moved to a new pool as the old one, though architecturally feted (it's now Grade I listed), was considered unsuitable, the pool being too shallow for them to dive and the concrete structure too hard on their feet.

Fox Photos/Hulton Archive

Teddy boys at Wembley 1972

Winklepickers, quiffs and rocking around the clock became fashionable again in the late 1960s and early '70s, when a new generation discovered the delights of rock 'n' roll. In the UK, George Lucas's teens-and-cars-and-rock movie *American Graffiti* was a runaway success, Chuck Berry topped the charts with his risqué novelty song 'My Ding-a-Ling' (its popularity boosted by Mary Whitehouse's attempt to get it banned) and, on 5 August 1972, Wembley Stadium hosted the Rock and Roll Revival Show. London's teddy boys came out in force to salute their '50s heroes: Bo Diddley, Bill Haley and the Comets, Little Richard, Jerry Lee Lewis and headliner Chuck Berry. The event was commemorated in Peter Clifton's film *The London Rock and Roll Show*.

Michael Webb/Keystone/Hulton Archive

Rustless diving suit
1925

Inventor Joseph Peress explains the workings of his Staybrite Silver Steel diving suit at the Olympia Shipping Exhibition. Key to the design were the articulated joints, which remained flexible and watertight at depths of up to 650 feet, but the suit was too heavy, at 500lbs, to be practical. Five years later Peress produced the Tritonia, the first functional atmospheric diving suit, made of lighter materials – but it wasn't until the 1960s, when North Sea oil exploration took off, that his ideas came to fruition. The inventor came out of retirement to help develop the much-used Jim suit (named after Peress's assistant, who had tested the original Tritonia), which was widely used around the world at depths beyond 1,900 feet.

E Bacon/Topical Press Agency/Hulton Archive

The Flip-Flap 1910

The Japan-British Exhibition was just one of an array of international showpieces held at White City at the beginning of the 20th century. Displays tended towards the educational, promoting the arts, culture, science and industry of various nations, but the fairground held just as much appeal for visitors, especially the Flip-Flap machine (visible in the background), its two slowly crossing arms providing spectacular views across London. It even inspired a popular music hall song, 'Take Me on the Flip-Flap', containing the refrain: 'Take me on the Flip-Flap, do, dear, do, it looks so lovely down below, so pay your money, and up you go, and though a queer sensation, you wish it would never stop, but down you slide, with a flip flap, flip flap.'

Hulton Archive

Titanic disaster 1912

The sinking of the *Titanic* hits the headlines of the *Evening News* on 16 April 1912, outside the Cockspur Street offices of the White Star Line, the shipping company that owned the cruise liner. The night before, the world's largest vessel went down after hitting an iceberg in the Atlantic, on her maiden voyage from Southampton to New York, with the loss of around 1,500 passengers and crew – thus becoming the world's most famous maritime disaster and setting in motion a century of myths, conspiracy stories, investigations, books, television programmes, films and seemingly never-ending interest. It was also just a couple of years before the outbreak of World War I; the newpaper boy pictured here, Ned Parfett, was killed during a German bombardment while serving in France, just days before the end of the war.

Topical Press Agency/Hulton Archive

War declared 1939

3 September 1939: a newspaper seller on the Strand carries a placard announcing the declaration of war, following Germany's invasion of Poland two days earlier. Prime Minister Neville Chamberlain announced the news to the nation by radio at 11.15am: 'This morning, the British Ambassador in Berlin handed the German Government a final note, stating that unless we heard from them by 11 o'clock that they were prepared at once to withdraw their troops from Poland a state of war would exist between us. I have to tell you now that no such undertaking has been received and that consequently this country is at war with Germany.' France declared war on the same day.

Central Press/Hulton Archive

Christmas party in Hoxton 1933

Father Christmas seems to have arrived by
lorry rather than sleigh at this party organised
by the Hoxton Market Christian Mission,
though the attentive crowd of local kids
don't seem to mind. The mission was a
soup kitchen and refuge for the poor of the
notoriously rundown district, doling out food
and boots to the hungry and the shoeless.
It was founded in 1881 by brothers John
and Lewis Burtt and based in Shaftesbury
House on Hoxton Market Square (now the
site of a Real Greek restaurant). The Burtts
had been brought up by another local charity
and educated at the Ragged School on
Curtain Road, having been discovered living
on the streets.
Fox Photos/Hulton Archive

Daily Express building 1935

One of London's finest art deco buildings, the Daily Express building at 120 Fleet Street was completed three years before this photo was taken. Designed by engineer Owen Williams and architects Ellis & Clarke, it was nicknamed the 'Black Lubianka' thanks to its glossy facade of black Vitrolite, glass and chromium strips, and was a deliberate move by press tycoon Lord Beaverbrook to outclass the *Daily Telegraph*'s newly built HQ just down the road. The gold and silver lobby, designed by Robert Atkinson, is a marvel of Thirties flamboyance with its starburst ceiling, travertine walls, wave-patterned floor in blue and black rubber, and curving serpent handrails. Evelyn Waugh immortalised the building as Copper House, home of the *Daily Beast*, in his novel *Scoop*. The *Daily Express* moved out in the 1980s, along with the rest of Fleet Street's journalists.

London Express/Hulton Archive

Building London's sewers 1862

London's sewer system owes its existence to Sir Joseph Bazalgette, seen here top right surveying works for the Northern Outfall sewer at Abbey Mills pumping station on the Isle of Dogs. The city's population had mushroomed in the first half of the 19th century, putting huge strain on its primitive infrastructure and leading to cholera outbreaks that killed more than 30,000. Matters culminated in the 'Great Stink' of 1858 when a hot summer made the stench of the Thames unbearable. Bazalgette was chief engineer of the newly established Metropolitan Board of Works, which proposed an extensive network of underground channels, low-level sewers behind specially built riverside embankments (the Victoria, Albert and Chelsea Embankments) and treatment works. In all, 1,000 miles of channels were built and by 1866 most of the city was connected to the new drainage system.

W Brown/Otto Herschan/Hulton Archive

Hangman's ropes 1948

This picture shows the special ropes made by the London firm John Edgington that were used in executions in Britain. Based in the Old Kent Road, Edgington had been the sole supplier of hangman's ropes since the 1880s; they also made tents, awnings and flags. Following Parliament's experimental five-year supension of the death penalty in 1948, *Picture Post* ran a story discussing the benefits of this new opportunity to delve into the mind of a killer after he had committed his crime; this photo accompanied the article, under the title 'A work that may be no longer required'. The last executions on British soil took place in 1964, but the final abolition of the death penalty did not come until 1969.

Haywood Magee/Picture Post/Hulton Archive

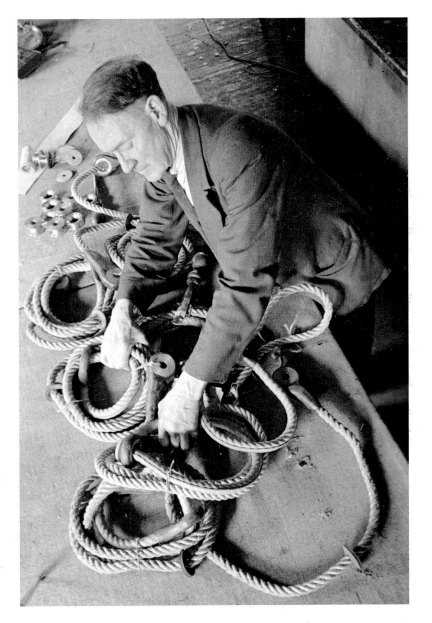

Searchlights over St Paul's 1943

St Paul's Cathedral became an important symbol of Britain's resilience during World War II, standing proud throughout the Blitz, despite being struck by a bomb in October 1940 that damaged its exterior walls and stained glass. (The windows were later replaced by plain glass, which would have pleased Sir Christopher Wren, who had specified clear glass in his original design). A similar image to this photograph was used on a 2005 stamp marking the 60th anniversary of the end of World War II, but omitting the beams at the side so that the remaining searchlights formed a V for Victory symbol.

Harry Shepherd/Fox Photos/Hulton Archive

Golden eagle in Regent's Park 1965

Goldie, London Zoo's golden eagle, became a national celebrity in March 1965 when he escaped while his cage was being cleaned. He evaded capture for almost two weeks, flying mainly around Regent's Park, but occasionally venturing into Camden Town and down Tottenham Court Road. Crowds flocked to the park to watch him flying between the trees. He ate one of the US Ambassador's ducks, attacked a couple of terriers and made newspaper headlines as he defeated attempts by police, firefighters and zoo keepers to catch him. He was eventurally lured back to the zoo with a dead rabbit. Goldie made a second bid for freedom in December of the same year, but was recaptured after only four days.

Terry Fincher/Express/Hulton Archive

Earl's Court Great Wheel
1895

The London Eye was by no means the first giant wheel to grace London's skyline. The Earl's Court Great Wheel, constructed in 1894-5, may be a clunkier affair than its 21st-century successor, but the basic design of cabins suspended from a bicycle-like spoked wheel is remarkably similar. Engineer Walter Bassett modelled it on George Washington Ferris's wheel for the 1893 World's Columbian Exposition in Chicago – the world's first observation wheel – but the British version was 35 feet taller, at 300 feet. Powered by two Robey steam engines, driving two 1,000-foot long chains, it held 1,200 people in 40 cars and took 20 minutes to revolve; at the top of the eight supporting legs were two recreation rooms. Ten of the cars were for first-class passengers, who paid twice the shilling fee of regular riders – but they were permitted to smoke while admiring the panoramic views. The wheel carried two and a half million passengers in its lifetime; it was scrapped in 1907 when it was no longer profitable. Bassett went on to build wheels in Blackpool and Paris, as well as the famous Reisenrad in Vienna that starred in *The Third Man* and is still in operation today.

General Photographic Agency/Hulton Archive

St Paul's during the Blitz 1941

The extent of the devastation inflicted on London during the Blitz is clear from this photo, looking north-east from St Paul's Cathedral. The sustained bombing campaign lasted from 7 September 1940 to 10 May 1941; for the first three months the capital was bombed virtually every night, the East End and docks area initially suffering most. The City was hit particularly hard on 29 December, when thousands of incendiaries and high-explosive bombs were dropped, resulting in the outbreak of 1,500 fires – the event was quickly dubbed the 'Second Great Fire of London'. St Paul's itself was spared chiefly because it was used as a navigation point by the German pilots.

Hulton Archive

Poll tax riots 1990

31 March 1990 was the day that marked the beginning of the end for Thatcherism. A cloud of black smoke hung over Trafalgar Square after an anti-poll tax rally in central London erupted into the worst riots seen in the city for a century. The West End resembled a war zone, as cars were overturned and set alight, restaurant windows smashed and businesses looted. Forty-five police officers were among the 113 people injured; more than 400 were arrested. Over 100,000 people turned out to protest against the tax, which was a levy on individuals regardless of means. Margaret Thatcher resigned as prime minister in November of the same year. Under John Major, the poll tax was replaced by the council tax.
Steve Eason/Hulton Archive

The first English airship 1902

Stanley Spencer (the aeronaut, not the painter) steers the first English airship on her 30-mile maiden flight from Crystal Palace to Harrow on 22 September 1902. Filled with hydrogen, the 88-foot long non-rigid craft (also known as a blimp) had a framework of ash and bamboo, a 35hp engine and room for only one passenger. The propeller was placed at the front rather than the rear (as in most airships), and if a large amount of gas escaped the whole thing was designed to fall to the ground like a parachute. Spencer made several exhibition flights at Crystal Palace and then constructed a larger version in 1903. There was a craze for airships in the first decade of the 20th century, with the French, Germans and Americans all competing to build bigger, better and faster designs.

London Stereoscopic Company/Hulton Archive

Sleeping in a playground 1934

Fresh air certainly has its benefits, but this north London school seems to be taking things a bit far by making its pupils have an open-air nap – hats, blankets and the watchful teacher's buttoned-up coat show how cold it is. It was all part of the drive against tuberculosis, which killed thousands each year until antibiotics and childhood vaccination became commonplace after World War II. Patients with TB were sent to sanitoriums for months, where they were encouraged to rest outside (regardless of the weather) as an 'air cure', and there were campaigns against public spitting, which was seen as a prime cause of infection.

Reg Speller/Fox Photos/Hulton Archive

Hyde Park 2007

Probably the most famous of London's green spaces, Hyde Park has been a royal park ever since it formed part of Henry VIII's vast hunting grounds, which stretched all the way from Kensington to Westminster. It has fulfilled many other roles over the years: as a place of public dissent and discussion, as a setting for rock concerts and grand exhibitions, as a boating, swimming, sunbathing and picnicking spot. But it's also simply a great place for a walk, its wide open spaces and criss-crossing paths – as this picture clearly shows – providing the perfect escape from the capital's concrete.

Mike Hewitt

Children with Hitler mask
1938

Children play in a King's Cross street wearing
popular masks of the time; it's just before
the outbreak of war, so it's not surprising
that baddies such as Hitler and Mussolini
feature, though film stars like Greta Garbo
and Anna May Wong also merit a mask.
Propaganda against the Nazis and in support
of the war effort was not restricted to adults,
of course; children were targeted too. Model
Spitfire and Hurricane fighter planes were
commonplace, a Hitler lookalike appeared in
Punch and Judy shows, boardgames included
Bomber Command (which invited players to
bomb Berlin), the Allies Dart Game apparently
used Hitler's face as a target (50 points for
hitting his moustache), and the *Dandy* comic
poked fun at the Germans with its depiction
of Hitler and Goering as 'Addy and Hermy,
the Nasty Nazis'.

William Vanderson/Fox Photos/Hulton Archive

London Olympics 1908

Crowds cheer Doranda Pietri of Italy as he runs through Harlesden (the clocktower in the background is still standing) during the marathon on 24 July 1908. Pietri ran the wrong way and collapsed several times in the Olympic Stadium at White City before winning the race, and was disqualified for being helped over the line by two officials – an image captured in a world-famous photograph. The gold medal was awarded to the second-placed American Johnny Hayes, but public sympathy was with Pietri, and the following day he was given a special gold cup by Queen Alexandra. Pietri is credited with popularising the marathon race, and the length of the modern marathon – 26 miles, 385 yards – was established at the London event, the result of the starting line being moved to Windsor Castle to allow the royal family a good view. London wasn't the original venue for the 1908 Olympics; the event was meant to be held in Rome, but the eruption of Mount Vesuvius in 1906, which devastated Naples, meant that funds intended for the Games were diverted to cope with the disaster.
Time Life Pictures/Mansell

London Olympics 1948

The 1948 Olympics Games was the first time that a photo-finish was used to determine the result of a race. In the 100 metres final, American Harrison Dillard and his compatriot Barney Ewell both clocked 10.3 seconds, but the photo-finish shows Dillard (at the bottom) just in front. This was also the first time the Olympics were televised (though few people in Britain owned a TV set). London had hosted the Games once before, in 1908; the outbreak of World War II meant that the events scheduled for 1940 and 1944 were cancelled. Fifty-nine nations took part in 1948 – but not Germany, Japan or the USSR. The capital was recovering from the aftermath of war and rationing was still in place, so athletes were housed in makeshift accommodation scattered across the city, and many competitors brought their own food.

PNA_Rota/Hulton Archive

Tower Bridge under construction 1892

Six years after building commenced, London's most famous bridge starts to take shape – though the steel frame looks rather naked without the Victorian Gothic stone cladding that gives the bridge its distinctive (some would say ridiculous) look. Horace Jones, the City architect also responsible for Smithfield, Billingsgate and Leadenhall Markets, had planned a plainer brick façade, but the design was changed after his death in 1887. A new bridge was required because of increased commerce in the East End, but shipping still needed to access the Pool of London between the Tower and London Bridge, hence engineer Sir John Wolfe-Barry's solution of a counterweighted bascule drawbridge. Although boat traffic is minimal these days, the bridge is still raised around 1,000 times a year.

London Stereoscopic Company/Hulton Archive

Skating in Wimbledon 1933

In the middle of an ice-skating boom in Britain, these women eschew the pleasures of the proliferating man-made rinks in favour of the great outdoors – a pond in Wimbledon, in this case. While the 20th century would never recreate the deep winter scenes of the 17th century, when skating on frozen ponds and fens was a huge craze and the Thames often iced over, outdoor skating was still very popular. More than 30 indoor rinks also opened in the 1930s, including the Queen's Ice Club in Bayswater and Streatham Ice Rink. Queen Victoria and Prince Albert had led the craze as far back as the 1840s, when her majesty had skates specially made and the prince consort almost came a cropper falling through the ice in the grounds of Buckingham Palace.

HF Davis/Topical Press Agency/Hulton Archive

Football fans at Stamford Bridge 1935

London derby games aroused as much passion in the past as they do now. Chelsea's official record attendance for a home game was set on 12 October 1935, when 82,905 squeezed into Stamford Bridge to watch the Blues play Arsenal – more fans had to balance precariously on billboards at the back of the ground to see the game (the Gunners won 5-2). Unofficially, the crowd was even larger, over 100,000, for Chelsea's encounter with Dynamo Moscow in 1945 – but neither figure will be bettered now that stadiums are all-seater. Opened in 1877, Stamford Bridge was originally used for athletics meetings; it became a dedicated football ground when Chelsea FC was founded in 1905. The stadium had only one covered terrace at first; a second, on the south side, was added in 1930: this became the famous Shed End, the favoured spot of Chelsea's most fervent and vocal supporters.

Popperfoto

Club Row pet market 1946

In the days before the RSPCA and animal rights, Club Row in Bethnal Green was the site of a famous and long-running pet market. The market probably originated with French Huguenot settlers in the 18th century, who brought their fondness for caged birds to the East End. Particularly popular were songbirds – goldfinches, bullfinches, thrushes, linnets – which were caught in the countryside around London. Also available were puppies, kittens, rabbits, reptiles, birds – and even rats, which were used as live bait in the dog fighting pits attached to many local pubs. The selling of animals at Club Row was finally banned in the 1980s.

Tony Linck/Time & Life Pictures

Gandhi in Canning Town 1931

Mohandas Gandhi paid two visits to London. In 1888, at the age of 19, he came to study law at UCL. On his return, in September 1931, he was no longer the young wannabe barrister in western clothes, but the Mahatma, the leader of the Indian independence movement, dressed in the traditional white *khadi* (homespun cloth) and sandals that symbolised his rejection of British domination. As sole representive of the Indian National Congress he was attending the Second Round Table Conference to discuss Indian home rule. Instead of staying in a fancy hotel, Gandhi chose to lodge amid the working classes of the East End, in Kingsley Hall, E3, run by his long-standing friends and social activists Doris and Muriel Lester. He spent 12 weeks at the hall – a blue plaque commemorates his visit – accompanied by a goat that provided him with milk. Gandhi's visit aroused considerable public interest; the East End turned out in force for a glimpse of the great man. Here, he's on his way to meet Charlie Chaplin, who was in town for the British premiere of *City Lights*.

London Express/Hulton Archive

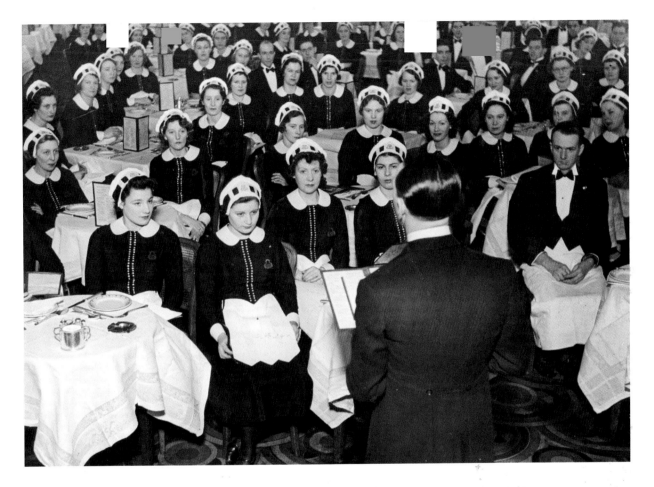

Lyons Corner House 1939

For the first half of the 20th century, Lyons was synonymous with a good cuppa. The company had tea shops all over the country, as well as three Corner Houses in London on Coventry Street, the Strand and Tottenham Court Road. These four- or five-storey emporiums, with food halls, hairdressing salons and theatre ticket agents as well as tea rooms, added a touch of grandeur to the tea-drinking experience, while the ranks of pristine, well-drilled young waitresses, known as 'nippies' – captured here by Bill Brandt for *Picture Post* – provided a dash of wholesome glamour. During the 1920s and '30s, the nippy's clean and respectable girl-next-door image achieved iconic status, becoming a familiar advertising tool across the land.

Bill Brandt/Picture Post/Hulton Archive

British
royalty 1935

The British royal family has never been very
good at relaxing in public, tending to look
stern, embarrassed or stiff, sometimes all
three – as seems to be the case in this
picture of Queen Mary, wife of George V,
with her second son, the Duke of York and
his wife, the Duchess of York (much loved
in later life as the Queen Mum). They're at
the British Industries Fair, presumably in
the toy department. A year later, the Duke
unexpectedly became King George VI on the
abdication of his brother, Edward VIII, over the
latter's determination to marry the American
divorcée Wallis Simpson. In a rare example of
voluntary press censorship, the public were
kept in the dark about the constitutional crisis
until the the abdication was announced.

Popperfoto

John, Yoko and Michael X 1970

Black power leader Michael X swaps a pair of Muhammad Ali's boxing shorts for the freshly cut hair of John Lennon and his wife Yoko Ono – the items were to be auctioned for charity. Michael X (born Michael de Freitas) was a pimp, drug dealer and rent collector for slum landlord Peter Rachman before becoming the self-appointed leader of London's black community in the 1960s, running a centre on Holloway Road called the Black House. A controversial figure, vilified in the mainstream press but supported by left-leaning celebrities, he was the first non-white to be imprisoned under the Race Relations Act (for advocating violence against black women who mixed with white men). Arrested for extortion in 1971, he fled to his native Trinidad, where he was hanged for murder a few years later.

Terry Disney/Express/Hulton Archive

Ice-cream seller in Putney 1932

The ice-cream trade in London has always been dominated by Italians. One of the first was Swiss-Italian immigrant Carlo Gatti, who set up a stall selling halfpenny ices in Hungerford Market in the late 1840s and is credited with introducing the ice-cream cart to the capital's streets. By the end of the 19th century there were some 900 ice-cream vendors in Holborn's Little Italy, known as Hokey Pokey men – probably a corruption of the Italian *Ocche poco*, which translates as 'Oh, how little', meaning cheap. The habit of licking ice-cream out of a small reusable dish, the 'penny lick', died out after the invention of the edible cone.

Central Press/Hulton Archive

George V's coronation 1911

With no television coverage (that would have to wait until George VI was crowned in 1937), but plenty of pomp and circumstance – and decorations galore – the coronation of George V on 21 June 1911 demanded a huge amount of preparation, not just for the coronation route but also along the much longer royal parade route the following day, as seen here at the Royal Exchange. On the left is the old Bank of England, designed by Sir John Soane, which was demolished in the 1920s to make way for the current building – an act described by Nikolaus Pevsner as 'the greatest architectural crime, in the City of London, of the 20th century'.

Hulton Archive

Post Office Tower 1964

The nearly completed Post Office Tower looms over Fitzrovia; at 620 feet high (including aerial) it was the tallest building in the capital until eclipsed by the Nat West Tower in 1981. The two observation decks and Butlins-run revolving restaurant (one complete revolution every 22 minutes) were very popular with the public until they were closed after an IRA bomb exploded in the toilets in 1971. Despite being one of London's most conspicuous and familiar landmarks, the telecommunications tower – still known by its original name though its proper title is the BT Tower – didn't officially exist until quite recently, being left off Ordnance Survey maps for security reasons.

Ted West/Central Press/Hulton Archive

Circus performers 1955

A very, very tall stiltwalker and a chubby clown make their way through the outskirts of London, en route to Tom Arnold's Christmas Circus at Harringay Arena. Impresario Tom Arnold, aka 'the King of Pantomime', didn't just deal in circuses: he put on ice spectaculars, plays, films, operas, revues and even rodeos, across Britain and abroad. Harringay Arena was a multipurpose venue too; constructed in 1936 (with a massive steel roof by Dorman & Long, builders of the Sydney Harbour Bridge), it was designed for ice-hockey, then very popular, but was also used for boxing, classical music, ballet and the American evangelist Billy Graham's first 'crusade' in the UK, in 1954. It was demolished in 1978.

Edward Tracey/BIPs/Hulton Archive

Franco-British Exhibition 1908

Lavish international exhibitions were all the rage in Edwardian London, and the place to see them was White City, a vast wonderland of halls and pavilions, all in an oriental style (and with white facades – hence the name) and connected by paths, bridges and waterways. Created by Hungarian-born entrepreneur Imre Kiralfy, the showgrounds opened in 1908 with the Franco-British Exhibition (alongside the first London Olympics), followed in quick succession by the Imperial International Exhibition (1909), the Japan-British Exhibition (1910), the Coronation Exhibition (1911), the Latin-British Exhibition (1912) and the Anglo-American Exhibition (1914). The site was used for making parachutes in World War II and later became the headquarters of BBC Television.

London Stereoscopic Company/Hulton Archive

Fog warning at South Woodford 1938

As the nickname Big Smoke attests, London's reputation for top-quality pea-soupers stretches back centuries. Fog or, more specifically, smog was caused by pollution from coal fires getting trapped near the ground by a mass of cold heavy air, so winter was the prime season. Disruption to rail and road services was commonplace, as evident here. The Great Smog in early December 1952 shrouded the capital in a poisonous black cloud for four days. It was so thick in places that people could not see their own feet, cattle at Smithfield were asphyxiated and theatres closed because nobody could see the stage. At least 4,000 people died as a direct result of the weather, though some estimates put the death toll as high as 12,000.

HF Davis/Topical Press Agency/Hulton Archive

Jarrow Crusade 1936

On 5 October 1936, 207 men set off from Jarrow on Tyneside to march almost 300 miles to London to bring attention to the extreme poverty and mass unemployment endured in the north-east. Carrying a petition with 11,000 signatures demanding government aid for Jarrow, they waved blue and white 'Jarrow Crusade' banners, sang to keep their spirits up and were given food and shelter by symphasisers en route. They arrived 25 days later, accompanied by local MP 'Red Ellen' Wilkinson, and held a rally in Hyde Park. Despite winning extensive public support – and becoming a landmark event in the labour movement – the march made little difference; although a shipbreaking yard and steelworks were set up in Jarrow a couple of years later, conditions remained bleak until World War II when rearmament kickstarted the area's industry.

E Dean/Topical Press Agency/Hulton Archive

First Aldermaston march 1958

On Good Friday 1958, following a rally in Trafalgar Square, thousands of protesters set off on a 50-mile trek to the atomic weapons research centre at Aldermaston near Reading. The Cold War was at its height, the British government had just carried out its first H-bomb tests in the Pacific, and the Campaign for Nuclear Disarmament had been founded a couple of months before. Parents carried toddlers, jazz musicians played and many marchers brandished placards bearing the newly created CND symbol (combining the semaphore signs for N and D). They walked through rain and sleet, staying in church halls and schools, arriving four days later, by which time the crowd had swelled to 9,000. The anti-nuclear movement was born.

Keystone/Hulton Archive

Paddington station 1910

This panorama of a busy Paddington station was one of more than 2,000 shot by Alfred Hind Robinson between 1903 and 1930, using the autotype process, a special form of carbon printing that was much loved by the Victorians. He travelled all over England, Scotland and Ireland and as far afield as northern Belgium and Holland, chiefly taking landscape and seaside panoramas with a clockwork Kodak camera, but he also shot castles, cathedrals, abbeys, bridges, racetracks, harbours and golf courses. In London, he covered popular tourist sights such as Hyde Park, Whitehall, Trafalgar Square and Big Ben, as well as Chelsea Football Club, Wembley Stadium and the 1911 Festival of Empire at Crystal Palace.

Alfred Hind Robinson/Hulton Archive

Balloon race at Hurlingham 1909

Ballooning became a popular sport for the upper classes in the early 20th century, with races frequently held by aeronautical clubs around the country. This point-to-point at Fulham's Hurlingham Club was won by John Dunville, of the Dunville Irish whiskey family, who broke several records in his day and won many trophies. The Hurlingham sports club, still a bastion of the elite, was founded in 1869 and became synonymous with the newly introduced game of polo. The club regularly held society balls and elaborate fetes, as well as pigeon shooting, archery, lawn tennis, croquet and car rallies.

Topical Press Agency/Hulton Archive

Procession in 'Little Italy' 1928

The focus of London's Italian community used to be not Soho but Clerkenwell, especially the area bounded by Clerkenwell Road, Farringdon Road and Rosebery Avenue, which was known as Italian Hill in the late 19th century. At the turn of the 20th century, there were around 11,000 Italians in the city, many employed as organ-grinders, ice-cream makers, knife-grinders and mosaic craftsmen. They also sold street food, especially chestnuts imported from northern Italy. The community began to disperse in the 1930s, many moving to Soho, where they replaced the previously dominant French residents. The annual procession of Our Lady of Mount Carmel was first held in Clerkenwell in the 1880s. It still takes place every July, organised by the Italian church of St Peter's on Clerkenwell Road.

London Express/Hulton Archive

VE Day 1945

On 8 May 1945, the official Victory in Europe day and the day after Germany's signing of the document of unconditional surrender, World War II ended. More than a million people, many dressed in red, white and blue and waving British and American flags, took to the streets of the capital, especially in the West End. Crowds gathered outside Buckingham Palace, where the Princesses Elizabeth and Margaret appeared on the balcony alongside King George VI and Queen Elizabeth – though the biggest roar of approval was for Winston Churchill, who announced the German surrender from the Ministry of Health in Whitehall. Fireworks and bonfires, singing and dancing, drinking and partying: London went mad with scenes of jubilation that would not be seen again until 21 years later when England won the World Cup.

Picture Post/Hulton Archive

Osmond mania 1975

Teenage girls in the early 1970s fell into two camps: those who adored Donny Osmond and those who would die for David Cassidy. War raged in the UK pop charts between the squeaky-clean, cherubic Mormon and the floppy-haired star of US TV show *The Partridge Family*, especially in 1972, when Donny's 'Puppy Love' and David's 'How Can I Be Sure' both spent weeks in the top slot. Donny won in the end, if only because he lasted longer, amassing 26 UK hits in five years, either solo or with his brothers in the Osmonds. The flares, tank tops, scarves and screaming teens were out in force in 1975 to greet the group's performance at Earl's Court.

Central Press/Hulton Archive

10 Rillington Place 1953

Policeman stand guard outside the Ladbroke Grove home of serial killer John Reginald Halliday Christie, who murdered at least six women, hiding three bodies in a bricked-up pantry in the kitchen, burying two in the garden and his wife under the floorboards in the front room. He was hanged at Pentonville Prison on 15 July 1953. Christie probably also murdered the wife and young daughter of Timothy Evans, who lived in the upstairs flat and had been executed for their murders in 1950 – a miscarriage of justice that later played a part in the abolition of the death penalty. Macabre sightseeing tours of the street (renamed Ruston Close) continued into the mid 1970s when it was knocked down to make way for the Westway; the site of 10 Rillington Place is now a garden.

Topical Press Agency/Hulton Archive

Bus in a bomb crater 1940

It may look like a toy, but this is a full-sized bus, wedged into the massive hole resulting from a direct hit on Balham tube station during the Blitz. On 14 October 1940, a bomb struck the road above the tube station, fracturing service pipes and damaging the Northern Line tunnel 30 feet below. Water and sewage flooded the low-lying station, where 500 people were sheltering; some escaped through the tunnel to the next station, but 68 died, including four Underground staff. It took three months to clear the debris and recover all the bodies.

Hampton/Hulton Archive

Doing the can-can 1951

A slice of Parisian life came to London in 1951 when the French-themed restaurant and nightclub Pigalle opened its doors, courtesy of Monsieur and Madame Gero. The audience was entertained by French songs by English impressionists, posh English girls doing cabaret and rather less posh English girls showing lots of leg as they danced the can-can, a menu in French and the distinctly un-French Max Bygraves. Sited in a former air-raid shelter (refurbished at a cost of £20,000), the Pigalle was intended to entertain visitors to the Festival of Britain; it didn't last, but its spirit lives again as the capital has seen a revival of burlesque in recent years (including a new Pigalle, in Piccadilly).
John Chillingworth/Hulton Archive

The Flesh is Weak 1956

'The shame of London exposed! … go home and warn your daughters!' screamed the tagline for this notorious British exploitation flick. The tale of a respectable girl lured into prostitution by a family of pimps (based on the real-life and exceedingly unpleasant Messina brothers gang) and eventually saved by an intrepid journalist, the film now seems pretty tame stuff. The good-looking but evil-hearted lead was played by John Derek, best known for his trio of lookalike sex-symbol wives (Ursula Andress, Linda Evans, Bo Derek), while director Don Chaffey was also responsible for the memorable spectacle of Raquel Welch in a fur bikini (in *One Million Years BC*). The Cameo Royal movie palace on the edge of Leicester Square was one of a string of sex cinemas in the area; all are long gone, with the Cameo being demolished in 1984 to make way for offices.

John Firth/BIPs/Hulton Archive

Caledonian Market 1935

Every Tuesday and Friday, the Metropolitan
Cattle Market in Islington gave over its square-
mile site of stalls and pens to the Caledonian
Market, where cash-strapped shoppers,
collectors and bargain-hunters could haggle for
everything from new and used clothing, shoes
and books to carpets and dartboards (a craze
in the mid '30s). Opened in 1855 by Prince
Albert, the cattle market enabled trading of
up to 15,000 livestock, but the bric-a-brac and
street market held more appeal for the general
public and was lucrative for vendors too; more
than 2,000 stallholders would pour through
the gates hoping to get a good pitch. At the
end of the war the market moved south of the
river, where it became the New Caledonian
or Bermondsey Market – and notorious for
fencing stolen goods.

A Hudson/Topical Press Agency/Hulton Archive

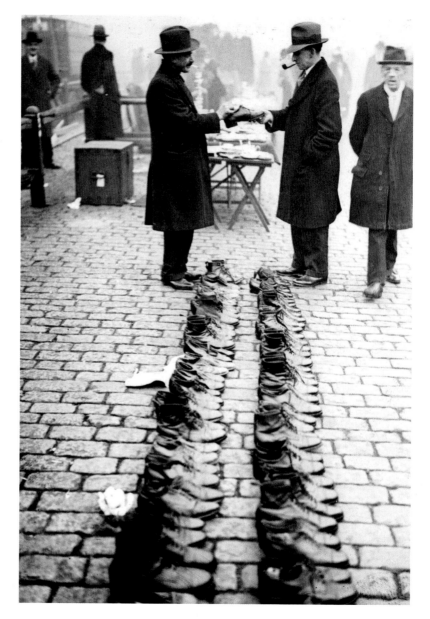

Lindbergh at Croydon Airport 1927

A crowd surrounds pioneering American aviator Charles Lindbergh as he arrives at Croydon Airport, shortly after completing the first solo transatlantic flight from New York to Paris in 1927. Lindbergh's achievement earned him $25,000 in prize money and worldwide fame, a combination that led to the kidnapping, ransom and murder of his infant son in 1932. The world's first purpose-built international airport, Croydon opened in 1920 and was London's main airport for 30 years; it also played a pivotal role in the Battle of Britain. Closed in 1959, it was paved over and turned into the notorious Roundshaw housing estate, although a few of the original buildings still exist and some of the street names – Lindbergh Road, Spitfire Road, Meteor Way, Vickers Close – are a reminder of its place in aviation history.

FPG/Time & Life Pictures/Hulton Archive

Boxing Krays 1950

It seems that the Kray brothers, celebrity gangsters of the 1960s, were never going to be far from the limelight. Growing up in Hoxton and Bethnal Green in the 1930s and '40s, twins Reggie (left) and Ronnie showed an early talent for violence. This picture was taken, with their adored mother Violet, when they were 16 and becoming keen and successful amateur boxers. It is said that neither lost a bout until they turned professional at the age of 19.

Fox Photos/Hulton Archive

A gas mask for babies 1939

This rather terrifying contraption is a gas mask specially designed for babies. Inside is Neville Mooney, the first baby born in London after the declaration of World War II. The government distributed 40 million masks in the months prior to the outbreak of war; while the adult masks were uncomfortable but effective, and children had 'Mickey Mouse' masks made of red rubber with white-rimmed eye pieces – an attempt to make them less scary – the full-body version for babies was air-tight and had to be continually hand-pumped to prevent suffocation. Intended for emergency use only, they were, fortunately, never needed.

Keystone/Hulton Archive

Punch and Judy show 1880

Punch and Judy have been entertaining Londoners for hundreds of years (Samuel Pepys recorded seeing a show in Covent Garden in 1662), but the puppet show hit its peak of popularity in Victorian times. Punchmen performed almost everywhere, by the seaside, at fairs, in front rooms, on city streets – as here, in Waterloo Place – attracting both young and old, rich and poor. Remove the onlookers and the scene looks very similar today: the buildings, towering Crimean War Memorial and even the streetlamps are all still in place. The circular negative (and thus print) was typical of early cameras; the most popular was George Eastman's Kodak camera introduced in 1888, which contained a roll of negative film sufficient for taking 100 circular photos, each about two-and-a-half inches in diameter. The camera was sent back to the company for processing, hence Kodak's motto: 'You press the button, we do the rest.'

Sean Sexton/Hulton Archive

Truman Brewery 1959

For generations the brick chimney of Truman's Black Eagle Brewery loomed over Spitalfields, and the smell of yeast and hops flavoured the streets for miles around. The area's connection with brewing dates back to the 17th century; the Truman Brewery, located halfway up Brick Lane, opened in 1724 and expanded rapidly, producing nearly half a million barrels of beer a year in the 1850s. By the 1870s, the firm – by then called Truman, Hanbury & Buxton – was the biggest brewery in the capital and the second biggest in the country. It stopped operating in 1988, but the buildings (including chimney) still play an important part in east London life thanks to the offices, bars, restaurants, art galleries, event spaces and markets now occupying the site.

Evening Standard/Hulton Archive

Battersea Pleasure Gardens 1956

The 1951 Festival of Britain wasn't all high culture on the South Bank, it also offered the lighter-hearted alternative of the Festival Pleasure Gardens in Battersea Park. The site included restaurants, cafés, a riverside theatre, bandstand and children's zoo amid flowerbeds planted in patriotic red, white and blue, but the funfair rides were the main attraction. Favourites included the the Big Dipper rollercoaster, the Water Chute (right) and the Rotor (below) – 'the world's greatest sensation' read the sign above the entrance. Riders were pinned to the wall of a large cylinder by centripetal acceleration as the floor fell away beneath them, while spectators could watch the resulting mayhem from viewing galleries. The Gardens were such a hit that, although intended to last only as long as the Festival, some exhibits remained for years. The fun finally ended in the mid 1970s following a fatal crash on the Big Dipper.

FPG/Hulton Archive
Bennett/Hulton Archive

Milkman on skis 1962

The winter of 1962/63, aka the Big Freeze of '63, was one of the coldest on record, with much of England under a thick blanket of snow from Boxing Day until early March. Temperatures hovered near or below zero for two months, lakes and rivers froze, and patches of ice even formed on the sea. Blizzards and freezing fog disrupted road and rail, airports closed and work was halted at the London docks. Children loved it because they could build igloos and the schools shut, but their parents had to cope with power cuts, fuel shortages, burst water mains and rocketing food prices. In London, mini icebergs floated down the Thames, people had to dig their way through snow drifts – and milkmen came up with ingenious ways of getting about.
Terry Fincher & Michael Stroud/Express/Hulton Archive

David Bowie and dog 1974

David Bowie poses nonchalantly with a scary-looking hound in a shoot for the artwork for the cover of his album *Diamond Dogs*. The pictures – by British photographer Terry O'Neill, who made his name in the 1960s and '70s for his photos of the Beatles, the Stones and the Who as well as Hollywood stars and the British royal family – were used as inspiration for the LP's iconic hybrid illustrations by Belgian artist Guy Peellaert. This particular photograph was a fluke, according to O'Neill: 'Suddenly this dog leaps up in the air, and thank God I had a wide-angle lens on, and it's just up there large as life… and Bowie didn't even move a hair.'

Terry O'Neill/Hulton Archive

Billingsgate Market 1935

Early morning mayhem as cartloads of fish arrive outside Billingsgate Market on Lower Thames Street. Famous for its foul smells and fouler language, Billingsgate had operated as a general market since the 11th century; in 1699 an Act of Parliament designated it 'a free and open market for all sorts of fish whatsoever'. The first purpose-built market opened in 1850, replaced in 1877 with the current building, designed by Corporation of London architect Sir Horace Jones. The flat leather 'bobbing' hats worn by the white-coated porters as they ferried boxes of fish into the market (pictured below, in 1942) were said to be modelled on the helmets worn by Henry V's bowmen at Agincourt; nowadays fork-lift trucks do the work. Running a bustling market in the heart of the busy City was a problem for a century, and in 1982 the market moved to the Isle of Dogs.

Popperfoto

Keystone Features/Hulton Archive

Building the Westway 1969

Not many roads can claim to have been immortalised in song, but the Westway isn't just any road; for many, it's the starting point of London proper. In 1969, its fame was centred around its scale and scope; building an eight-lane motorway over densely populated Victorian neighbourhoods necessitated the kind of planning that wouldn't be seen again until the regeneration of Docklands. Here, at the Western Avenue extension, construction took place over three levels. The road won a place in lyrical history, thanks to the Clash's 'London's Burning'.

Peter Trulock/Fox Photos/Hulton Archive

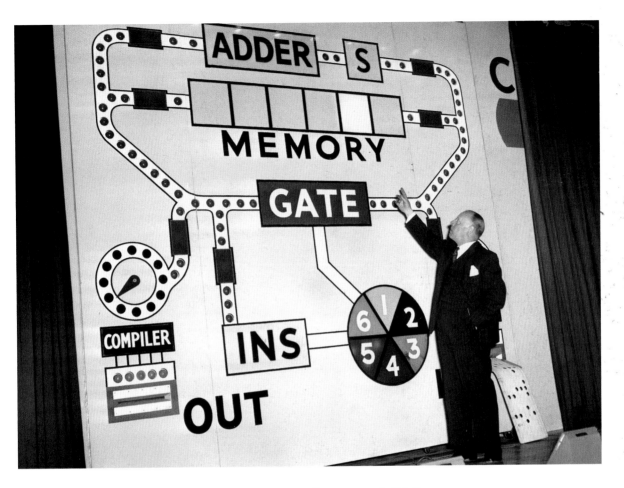

How a computer works 1959

Though mechanical adding devices had been around since 1900, by 1959 the race was on to develop a practical electronic calculator. Work on mainframe computers in the late 1940s and '50s had led the way for IBM to develop the first commercial computer in 1954, though it was housed in several cabinets and cost $80,000. The first electronic calculator was developed in 1961 and by 1970 had become pocket-sized, though it wasn't until 1976 that the pocket calculator became a commonly affordable item. Here, Dr HA Thomas of Unilever delivers the 1959 Faraday Lecture at the Royal Festival Hall, explaining how a 'computer' works. Numbers go in on a punched card on the right, and the solution emerges on the left.

Jimmy Sime/Central Press/Hulton Archive

Premiere of Modern Times 1936

Workmen put the finishing touches to a huge neon sign on the Tivoli cinema in the Strand, in preparation for the UK premiere on 11 February 1936 of Charlie Chaplin's *Modern Times*. The movie was significant for various reasons: it marked the last appearance of Chaplin's most famous creation, the Little Tramp – this time facing the perils of factory machinery, poverty, starvation and Depression unrest – and it was the first time Chaplin 'spoke' in one of his films. At one point, the tramp, hired as a waiter, sings in mock Italian gibberish. Although talking pictures had been established for almost a decade by 1936, Chaplin knew that silent pantomime was what gave his films universal appeal – 'I know that I cannot use dialogue', he said. The Tivoli was demolished in 1957.

David Savill/Topical Press Agency/Hulton Archive

Elephant and a tram 1936

Elephants on the streets of London were, surprisingly, not such a rare sight in the years leading up to World War II. This one, getting friendly with a tram driver on Grays Inn Road, was probably appearing in a theatre production, where elephants had been popular for almost a century; as far back as 1846 the City of London Theatre in Shoreditch borrowed two elephants from a Paris circus to appear in a play that had been specially devised around the tricks they performed. The use of live animals in theatre goes back even further – to 1788, when actor and theatre manager John Kemble (brother of famous actress Sarah Siddons) introduced them to the London stage.

Fox Photos/Hulton Archives

Funeral of Blair Peach 1979

Blair Peach, a New Zealander teaching in London, was killed during an anti-National Front demonstration in Southall on 23 April 1979. Violence broke out between the Metropolitan Police's much-despised Special Patrol Group and anti-racism protesters; more than 40 people, including 21 police, were injured and hundreds arrested. Despite numerous eyewitness reports that Peach had been hit over the head by a policeman, no public inquiry was held, the inquest reported a verdict of misadventure and no one was charged with his murder. A public outcry ensued and the event became a long-running symbol of establishment injustice and police brutality, inspiring Linton Kwesi Johnson's passionate protest song 'Reggae Fi Peach'.

Mike Lawn/Evening Standard/Hulton Archive

Bolan's Mini 1977

Glam rock sensation Marc Bolan caused a final sensation on 16 September 1977 when he died in a purple Mini being driven by his girlfriend Gloria Jones as they headed home from Morton's in Berkeley Square, two weeks before his 30th birthday. Bolan was in the passenger seat – he'd never learned to drive, fearing a premature death in a car accident – and was killed instantly when the speeding vehicle crashed into a sycamore on Queens Ride, on the edge of Barnes Common. The site immediately became a place of pilgrimage for Bolan fans; it was officially recognised by the English Tourist Board after the T-Rex Action Group began to look after it, TAG founder Fee even paying for a bronze bust to be erected at the site in 2002.

Maurice Hibberd/Evening Standard/Hulton Archive

Elephant tusks in Docklands
1948

An inspector checks the quality of elephant tusks in Docklands prior to the annual ivory auction. London was the centre of the international ivory trade for years, attracting buyers from across the globe. Ivory House, a warehouse in St Katharine's Dock (now used mainly for flats), was built in 1858-60 specifically for dealing with the huge quantities of ivory that arrived at the Port of London each year: up to 200 tonnes – amounting to 5,000 dead elephants, plus assorted walruses.

Popperfoto

Hampstead Heath funfair 1936

The funfair held on Hampstead Heath has been thrilling locals and holiday-makers since late Victorian times. In 1910 the event was so popular that a crowd of more than 200,000 attended – a vast hedonistic congregation for those days. Originally held annually over the Easter holiday weekend, the fair still appears each year at Easter and now also on the other bank holidays in May and August. The much-loved swingboats, however, are no longer a feature, having been replaced with more modern and considerably more white-knuckle attractions.
E Dean/Hulton Archive

End of the Boer War 1902

On Peace Day, 31 May 1902, thousands of people poured on to the streets around Mansion House to celebrate the end of the Second Boer War. Considered a great victory at the time, the war later came to be seen as a particularly shameful episode in British history. The so-called 'Last of the Gentlemen's Wars' was anything but; in a bid to control the guerrilla tactics of the warring Afrikaners, British troops under Lord Kitchener detained more than 116,000 people – almost a quarter of the entire Boer population – in overcrowded and unhygienic concentration camps (the first use of the term), leading to the deaths of more than 26,000 women and children.

London Stereoscopic Company/Hulton Archive

Street performers 1955

Modern-day buskers are an unimaginative lot compared to their predecessors. Here we have dancer and organist Mick and Mike (according to the chalk sign on the side of their barrel organ) – and what might be a monkey or a particularly ornate hat – drumming up custom on a West End street. Things were even more elaborate in earlier years. A *Picture Post* article from 1938 describes the buskers playing nightly to London theatregoers; as well as fiddlers and banjo players, there was an acrobat, a juggler, a paper tearer, 'Putty' the clay modeller, 'Sketchy' the quick-fire cartoonist and 'Jock the Dancer', who, aged 73, perfomed the Lancashire clog dance and Scottish reels.

Slim Aarons/Hulton Archive

Twiggy at Biba 1973

Twiggy sits alone in the Rainbow Room of Big Biba, formerly the art deco Derry and Toms department store on Kensington High Street. Barbara Hulanicki's ground-breaking fashion label started as a mail order service in 1964; the company opened its first shop on Abingdon Road in Kensington, then in 1965 moved to the first of three locations on Kensington High Street. Yoko Ono, Cathy McGowan, Brigitte Bardot, Mia Farrow, Julie Christie and Barbra Streisand were regular customers. Big Biba sold cosmetics and household goods as well as the smock dresses, velvet trouser suits, miniskirts, suede boots and boas that had made Biba the must-have look of the Swinging Sixties (and paved the way for the cheap, disposable high-street fashion of today). But more people came to gawp at the huge store's glamorous interiors than to buy, and the recession of the early '70s didn't help: Biba folded after just two years.

Justin de Villeneuve/Hulton Archive

Tate Gallery 1963

This weirdly distorted picture – of people going into the Tate Gallery (now Tate Britain) – was taken by American photographer Arthur Fellig, better known as Weegee. He made his name as the definitive New York tabloid photographer in the 1930s and '40s, scouring the city by night with a darkroom in the trunk of his car and a police radio always on to ensure he was first to arrive at the latest murder, disaster or accident. His book of photographs, *Naked City*, inspired the 1948 film noir of the same name, and he was also a consultant on Stanley Kubrick's *Dr Strangelove*. In the 1950s he began experimenting with photo distortions (made in the darkroom or by shooting through a prism) and travelled across Europe, working for the *Daily Mirror* and on assorted photography, book and film projects. He died in 1968.

Arthur Fellig/International Centre of Photography/Hulton Archive

Monkeys at London Zoo 1952

At the time this photo of exuberant rhesus monkeys was taken, London Zoo was about to celebrate 125 years in business. The zoo was the brainchild of Sir Stamford Raffles, founder of Singapore, who set up the Zoological Society of London shortly before his death (of apoplexy) in 1826. The zoo itself was inaugurated in Regent's Park two years later. Originally open only to members of the ZSL, the zoo didn't allow the general public in until 20 years later, in a bid to raise funding. As well as being the first scientific zoo – Charles Darwin was a regular visitor – it was the first public institution to have a reptile house (1849), an aquarium (1853), an insect house (1881) and a children's zoo (1938).

William Vanderson/Fox Photos/Hulton Archive

Foyles bookshop 1958

Open since 1906 at its current address (113-119 Charing Cross Road), Foyles has been famous over the decades not only for its size and huge stock (it was once the biggest bookshop in the world), but also for some pretty idiosyncratic business practices that led one commentator to compare it to Kafka going into the book trade. Books, both second-hand and new, were at one time categorised by publisher rather than genre or author, and house rules that prohibited sales staff from handling money meant that customers had to queue up three times in order buy a book. These days the place is a bastion of independent bookselling, hosting (as it has done since 1930) literary luncheons and evening events and winning both academic and independent bookseller awards.

Rosemary Matthews/Hulton Archive

London's last horse-drawn tram 1913

The capital's horse-drawn trams rarely looked as bare as this one; their elegant sparseness was often hidden by yards of advertising hoardings along the sides and top of the vehicle, and they were usually packed with working-class Londoners who preferred them to the buses, which didn't run as early in the morning and were more expensive. The first horse-drawn tram appeared around 1870; five years later there were 350, serving most main roads except in the City and Westminster where they were banned. Each tram needed a team of about 11 horses to keep it running; the effort of pulling the heavy tramcar meant an animal only lasted about four years. The arrival of the electric tram at the turn of the 20th century signalled the demise of the horse-drawn version.

Hulton Archive

The Golden Arrow 1929

Looking impossibly futuristic next to a London bus, the Batmobile-like Golden Arrow is en route to Selfridges. A few weeks earlier, on 11 March 1929, Major Henry Seagrave had smashed the land speed record in it, reaching a staggering 231.446mph on the sands at Daytona, Florida. Two years earlier, he'd been the first to break the 200mph barrier. The 1920s and '30s were the golden age of speed records and Seagrave was one of racing's royalty, alongside Englishman Malcolm Campbell, Welshman Parry Thomas and American Ray Keech. Designed by JS Irving, the Golden Arrow was a revolutionary machine. Powered by a 930hp, 24-litre, 12-cylinder Napier Lion aeroplane engine, its aerodynamic aluminium body (painted gold) was almost 28 feet long; the underside was shaped like an aircraft wing in reverse, to keep it pinned to the ground. Seagrave's record lasted barely two years. Campbell hit 246.09mph in his revamped Bluebird in 1931, but by then Seagrave had joined the long list of speed record casualties – he was killed on Lake Windermere in 1930 while attempting to break the water speed record. Petrolheads can see the car in all its glittering glory at the National Motor Museum at Beaulieu.

Fox Photos/Hulton Archive

Microcar at Piccadilly Circus 1958

Dwarfed by a bus (and even by a moped), a Brütsch Mopetta negotiates the traffic at Piccadilly Circus. Very, very small cars were all the rage in Britain in the 1950s and early '60s, mainly because they were so cheap. The Heinkel Kabine (the original bubble car), the Messerschmitt KR200 and the BMW Isetta were particularly popular, though there was a bewildering variety of models. Stuttgart-based Brütsch specialised in microcars, churning out 11 different designs in the 1950s, though none was put into mass production. The single-seater, three-wheeler Mopetta had a 50cc engine, a roadster-style fibreglass body (only 67 inches long) and a top speed of 28mph. Although it was advertised as costing £200, only 14 were built – so Londoners never got the chance to drive to work in an egg.

Rosemary Matthews/BIPs/Hulton Archive

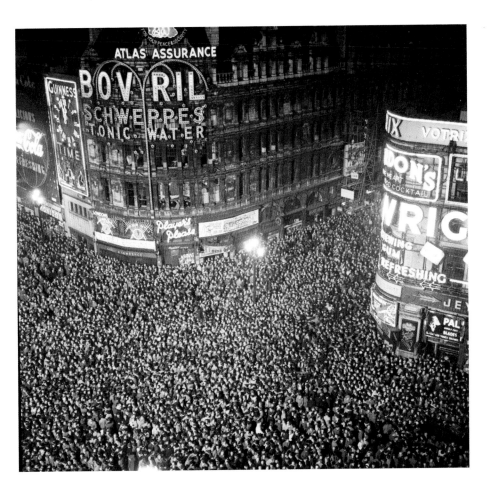

New Year's Eve 1954

Thousands of revellers wait for New Year to strike on the Guinness clock in Piccadilly Circus, one of London's most popular – and brightly lit – meeting points. Somewhat ironically, given the current climate of rampant consumerism, the neon advertising for which the Circus is famous was considerably more pervasive in the 1950s than it is today, with illuminated hoardings (first introduced in 1910) covering most of the building facades around the road junction. Nowadays, only one building is lit up, in the north-western corner between Shaftesbury Avenue and Glasshouse Street, and neon has been replaced by LED video technology. Coca-Cola is the only advertiser from the '50s that still occupies a space.

Harry Kerr/BIPs/Hulton Archive

Stunt plane
1930

A stuntman takes flight in what looks like
a streamlined bathtub with wheels at
Alexandra Palace in August 1930.
Miraculously, as the accompanying pictures
show, he survived this death-defying feat,
landing safely on a mattress about 20 feet
away from the steeply angled launch ramp.
Unfortunately, the reason for this remarkable
act of derring-do has been lost.

Fox Photos/Hulton Archive

Squat in Clerkenwell 1971

Clerkenwell was a very different place in the early 1970s, as this picture shows. A tenement building on Clerkenwell Road has been turned into a squat and daubed with some – now brilliantly dated – graffiti. Note the request for 'free pot/acid', salute the slogan 'Love your fellow man and give him a home', applaud the sheer staying power of 'Pigs out' and remember that the swastikas are of the Buddhist and Hindu, rather than Nazi, variety. Clerkenwell was a fine place for a squat, not only because of the number of empty and neglected buildings at the time; it's long been a home to revolutionaries, and Lenin edited the Communist newspaper *Iskra* just around the corner at 37A Clerkenwell Green, now home to the Marx Memorial Library.

Sydney O'Meara/Evening Standard/Hulton Archive

The Daleks invade the West End 1965

Lurking menacingly outside a phone box, the Daleks have landed in the West End to star in a stage play, *The Curse of the Daleks*, at Wyndham's Theatre. Written by Terry Nation (creator of the Daleks, as well as cult TV series *Survivors* and *Blake's 7*) and aimed at kids, it didn't include the Doctor or the TARDIS and only ran for a month. The first episode of the TV series *Doctor Who* was shown on BBC on 23 November 1963, with William Hartnell playing the Doctor; his arch-enemies the Daleks (supposedly intended as an allegory of the Nazis) appeared a month later in the second serial. The famous all-electronic theme music was created by Delia Derbyshire of the BBC's pioneering Radiophonic Workshop.

R McPhedran/Express/Hulton Archive

Bunny Girls in Park Lane 1976

Bunny Girls arrived in London in 1965, when Hugh Hefner opened his Playboy Club and casino at 45 Park Lane, following the liberalisation of the UK gambling laws. The club tallied with the liberated mood of the Swinging Sixties and became a celebrity hangout, though the Playboy empire was – and still is – also a frequent target for feminists and anti-porn campaigners. The Bunny Girls' costume, inspired by the tuxedo-wearing Playboy rabbit symbol and considered the ultimate in sexy glamour at the time, consisted of a satin corset, fluffy tail, headband with ears, and four-inch heels. It was excruciatingly uncomfortable, forcing wearers to bend at the knees, not the waist – the so-called 'bunny dip'. The club closed in 1981 when Playboy's gaming licence was revoked.

Aubrey Hart/Evening Standard/Hulton Archive

Debutantes in Piccadilly 1955

The peculiar practice of putting Britain's latest generation of upper-class gals into ball gowns and introducing them to the Queen as part of their launch into society – and into the arms of the country's most eligible young aristocrats – was still going strong in 1955, as it had been for 200 years. It would cease three years later, when changing trends deemed such rites of passage outmoded. The debs' season, essentially a round of parties, teas and social events, still takes place, but the girls no longer meet the monarch, and their fate is likely to be very different to that of most of the girls seen here on their way to a photoshoot in Hyde Park ahead of the annual Berkeley Debutantes Ball.

Central Press/Hulton Archive

Dancing bear 1900

This snapshot of a performing bear on an anonymous London street was taken by Paul Martin, one of the pioneers of candid photography. Born in France in 1864, he emigrated to England with his family in 1873. He took up photography as a hobby, using the new hand-held 'Facile' camera – disguised as a parcel – to capture informal shots of people on the streets of London and holidaying at the seaside. He also published a series of night shots of the capital, 'Around London by Gaslight', in the magazine *Amateur Photographer* in 1896. Martin turned professional, setting up his own studio and winning numerous awards from the Royal Photographic Society, but it was his pictures of everyday life – casual, naturalistic, revealing: the antithesis of po-faced Victorian studio portraits – that led Cecil Beaton to nickname him 'the Charles Dickens of photography'.

Paul Martin/Hulton Archive

Flooding in Rotherhithe
1928

The flood that hit the capital in the early hours of 7 January 1928 was the worst London has experienced to date. A combination of a sudden thaw, violent storms and a huge spring tide resulted in the Thames bursting its banks from the City of London and Southwark as far west as Putney and Hammersmith. Serious damage also occurred downriver, in Greenwich and Woolwich. The Houses of Parliament were flooded, as were tube stations and both Blackwall and Rotherhithe Tunnels. The normally dry moat of the Tower of London filled up for the first time in 80 years. A section of Chelsea Embankment collapsed at Millbank, and low-lying parts of town such as Rotherhithe were particularly badly affected. Fourteen people died – many drowning as they slept in basement rooms – and thousands were made homeless. Various measures were enacted to prevent a similar disaster, including raising the embankment walls, but the idea of a barrier across the river was rejected because of the effect it would have on shipping; the Thames Barrier didn't open until 1984.

Topical Press Agency/Hulton Archive

Renaming a tube station
1937

A London Underground worker replaces the sign at Post Office tube station with its new name, St Paul's, on 1 February 1937. Opened by the Central Railway Line in 1900, the station was originally named after the headquarters of the General Post Office on adjacent St Martin's le-Grand rather than the prominent landmark to its south, probably to avoid confusion with the nearby St Paul's overground station. When that became Blackfriars, the way was clear for Post Office to change its name too. The Underground's nomenclature has experienced some frenzied toing and froing, particularly in its early years. For example, Charing Cross opened in 1907, was renamed Charing Cross (Strand) in 1914, became Strand in 1915, closed in 1973 and then reopened – as Charing Cross again – in 1979. Oxford Street station lasted less than a year, turning into Tottenham Court Road in 1908 when the original Tottenham Court Road became Goodge Street. And so it continues to this day, mainly to make life easier for inattentive Londoners and visitors bewildered by same-named stations.

Topical Press Agency/Hulton Archive

Fulham football fans
1957

Freda and Frank Hearn's stylish monochrome look may appear to be at least ten years ahead of its time, but the duo are simply decked head to toe in the black and white of their beloved Second Division Fulham FC as they wait to board a train to a third-round FA Cup tie against Ipswich. Women and children attended games regularly in the '50s; average attendance at First Division matches was 50,000, entrance cost about 10p, or 20p for a seat in a stand at Craven Cottage, and players' fees were less than astronomical – even stars like Stanley Matthews could expect to earn no more than £17 a week. Fulham beat Ipswich 3-2, but went out in the next round to Blackpool, who thrashed them 6-2.

William Vanderson/Fox Photos/Hulton Archive

Gas attack practice 1937

Not an army of mutant monsters on the rampage, but some of London's telephone operators and engineers during a pre-war training session on gas attacks. Poison gas had been used extensively (by both sides) in World War I, and the government fully expected chemical warfare to be a feature of air raids on British cities. Millions of masks were handed out in the build-up to war, with special versions devised for workers in key areas such as telecommunications. Drills at work and school were common, though they didn't endear the populace to the masks, which were hot, uncomfortable and smelled unpleasantly of rubber and disinfectant. In the end, they were never needed as no gas attack was launched.

Harry Todd/Fox Photos/Hulton Archive

Trellick Tower 1972

Architect Ernö Goldfinger's Trellick Tower on Goldborne Road, just after it was finished in June 1972. By then, high-rise flats had fallen out of favour as a solution to Britain's post-war housing crisis, and tower blocks were unpopular with both the public and politicians. Goldfinger was a key figure in the development of the modern movement in Britain, but his uncompromising Brutalist style was dogged with controversy for most of his life – though nowadays Trellick Tower is a west London landmark, its flats highly sought after. He designed housing, schools, offices and shops in the capital, as well as headquarters for the Communist Party, the Elephant & Castle shopping complex and his own house in Willow Road, Hampstead. Ian Fleming named his most famous Bond villain after him, much to the architect's annoyance.

Peter Trulock/Fox Photos/Hulton Archive

Hyde Park free concert 1971

In the spirit of the age, Hyde Park hosted a series of free concerts between 1968 and 1971, where high-profile bands such as Pink Floyd and Soft Machine would entertain the masses. History has dictated that the most famous of these is the Rolling Stones' appearance on 5 July 1969, just after the death of their guitarist Brian Jones – though many who were in the audience that day report that the band's performance was underwhelming. The young bongo-player pictured here in beads, kaftan and directional haircut is part of the crowd who came to see Grand Funk Railroad, Head Hands and Feet and headline act Humble Pie. Reviews suggest Humble Pie's performance, their first in the UK for some time, was a triumph, though the ethos of peace and love was marred by Hells' Angels charging the crowd on their 'hogs'.

Central Press/Hulton Archive

Fortune-telling robot 1934

An expectant crowd gathers around a fortune-telling robot at Selfridges. The obsession with walking, talking, thinking mechanical creatures started in the 1920s, when Czech playwright Karel Capek coined the term 'robot' in his 1921 play *RUR* (Rossum's Universal Robots), and the beautiful female robot Maria appeared in Fritz Lang's silent movie masterpiece *Metropolis*. A flood of science fiction pulp magazines appeared in the '30s, alongside Aldous Huxley's futuristic novel *Brave New World* and the first Flash Gordon comic strip, which inspired three Flash Gordon films later in the same decade. American corporation Westinghouse exhibited a seven-foot-high mechanical humanoid Elektro and his robot dog Sparko at the 1939 World's Fair in New York. Elektro could walk, talk, count, distinguish between red and green (with his photoelectric 'eyes') and even smoke a cigarette.

London Express/Hulton Archive

The siege of Sydney Street 1911

In December 1910 three policemen were killed by three Russian anarchist suspects in a burglary at a Houndsditch jewellery shop, setting the scene for one of London's most famous battles two weeks later. Around 1,000 police and troops – as well as Winston Churchill, then home secretary (at the front, in the top hat) – engaged in a lengthy confrontation with the men at 100 Sydney Street, eventually killing two of them. Twenty years later, the event was reproduced by Alfred Hitchcock in his 1934 film *The Man Who Knew Too Much*. While it's a treasured part of East End folklore, the siege of Sydney Street was barely a siege at all, lasting less than 24 hours, and certainly nothing compared to the Hackney siege of 2003, when Jamaican gunman Eli Hall held off police for 15 days.

Popperfoto

Churchill's funeral 1965

On a bitterly cold Saturday, 30 January 1965, thousands line the streets as the gun carriage bearing Winston Churchill's coffin approaches St Paul's Cathedral. The wartime prime minister, who died aged 90, was the only commoner awarded a state funeral in the 20th century. After the service, attended by representatives of 113 countries, the cortege headed though the City to Tower Pier, from where the coffin was taken by barge along the Thames to Waterloo Station and finally by train to Bladon parish churchyard in Oxfordshire. Millions around the world watched the ceremony on television (BBC, black and white, commentary by Richard Dimbleby); for many, the most moving scenes were when the cranes of Docklands dipped in respect as the coffin passed by on the river.

Fox Photos/Hulton Archive

First FA Cup Final at Wembley 1923

The first event scheduled for the newly completed Wembley Stadium nearly didn't happen. Thousands of fans turned up for the FA Cup Final between Bolton Wanderers and West Ham United on 28 April 1923, rushed the ticket gates, burst the barriers and flooded the pitch, making it impossible for the match to start. Mounted police had to be summoned to push the crowds back to the touchlines; PC George Scorey and his horse, Billy, were particularly visible, resulting in the game's nickname, the 'White Horse Final'. The match finally kicked off after a 45-minute delay, with an estimated 200,000 fans squeezed into the stadium – 75,000 more than it was designed to hold. 'Wembley Stadium stormed by excited Cup Final crowds' screamed the front page of the *Sunday Pictorial* the following morning. Bolton Wanderers won 2-0, and the Wembley authorities decided that subsequent Cup Finals should be 'all ticket' affairs.

Central Press/Hulton Archive

Platform shoes 1972

The current penchant for shoes as sculpture is nothing new; platform shoes with eight-inch heels, such as these exhibited at the 1972 Spring Shoes Exhibition, were then all the rage in London fashion. They were refreshingly non-gender-specific (check out the footwear adopted by Elton John and Kiss at the time) and came decorated with all manner of celestial and natural motifs in myriad colours and materials. Most of all, they soared higher than shoes had ever gone before – up to 11 inches – so much so that the medical profession felt compelled to issue warnings about spine damage to those wearing them.

Frank Barratt/Hulton Archives

George V and Oxo 1935

Looking more as if they're hanging around for the bus than making history, King George V and Queen Mary are, in fact, waiting for the royal coach to collect them during celebrations for the king's Silver Jubilee. What's most striking are the large billboards behind the royal entourage – three for now-forgotten cigarette brands, one for Oxo. The Liebig Extract of Meat Company's beef stock cube was also celebrating its own quarter century, having appeared first in 1910. At the end of the '20s, the firm had taken over a former power station on the South Bank, rebuilding it in art deco style. When Liebig was refused permission to erect illuminated ads on the tower, it added a trio of windows on each side that just happened to be in the shape of a circle, a cross and a circle – thus creating one of London's most popular landmarks, the Oxo Tower.

London Express/Hulton Archive

Arsenal fans at Waterloo station 1932

These cheery-looking fans are about to catch a train for an FA Cup tie against Portsmouth at Fratton Park. Shiny shoes, suits and ties, assorted headgear, rosettes and football rattles are de rigeur (if only their modern-day counterparts would dress so smartly) – though it looks as if the letters spelling out ARSENAL were added later. They have much to be happy about: not in the 1932 season, actually, which was a disappointment as the Gunners finished as runner-up in both the league and FA Cup, but Arsenal dominated English football throughout the 1930s, winning a grand total of five league titles and two FA Cup championships.

SR Gaiger/Hulton Archive

Millennium projects 2001

Among the high-profile schemes in London marking the advent of the millennium were Tate Modern and the Millennium Bridge, both of which opened in 2000. The gallery created by architects Herzog & de Meuron out of Sir Giles Gilbert Scott's former Bankside power station was an immediate sensation, attracting five million visitors in its first year, while the bridge, designed by Foster & Partners and sculptor Anthony Caro, had a distinctly wobblier start. It closed two days after opening, when the structure started swaying alarmingly – an unforseen effect of the huge number of people using it. Following modifications by its engineer Arup, it reopened in 2002.

Tom Stoddart/Hulton Archive

Battersea Power Station 1934

So iconic is the profile of Battersea Power Station's four chimneys that it is hard to imagine that there were originally just two. The first phase of the development, Station A, opened in 1933, but it wasn't until 1953 that Station B, on the western side, was completed. At full capacity the station provided a fifth of London's electricity and much local employment. The original architect was K Theo Halliday, replaced early on in the project by the much more high-profile Sir Giles Gilbert Scott, architect of Bankside Power Station (now Tate Modern), Liverpool Cathedral, William Booth College and the classic red phone box. The steel-framed, brick-clad structure is reckoned to be the largest brick building in Europe, and on plan it could accommodate St Paul's Cathedral without it touching the sides. The art deco turbine hall of Station A was lined with Italian marble and its control room was so splendid that operators had to wear felt-soled shoes to protect the polished parquet floor.

Fox Photos/Hulton Archive

Jumbo the elephant 1870

This imposing pachyderm, pictured at London Zoo with his long-term keeper Matthew Scott, is the reason that the word 'jumbo' entered the English language. Born in the French Sudan in 1861, he was captured and shipped to the Jardin des Plantes in Paris, then transferred to London Zoo in 1865, where the staff called him Jumbo – a name that probably derives from one of two Swahili words, *jambo* ('hello') or *jambe* ('chief'). He was at least 11 foot tall, and the star attraction for years. But Jumbo grew increasingly temperamental as he aged, and when American showman Phineas Taylor Barnum, owner of one of the world's most successful travelling circuses, offered to buy him in 1881 for £2,000, the zoo agreed. A public outcry ensued and children wrote anguished letters to Queen Victoria, but in 1882 Jumbo left for the States by steamship. He became the highlight of the Barnum & Bailey Circus, touring the US and Canada, until he was hit and killed by a train in Ontario in 1885.

London Stereoscopic Company/Hulton Archive

Serpentine Lido 1937

The golden age of outdoor swimming was the 1930s, when the London County Council built 50 lidos across the capital to promote healthy living and provide a beachlike experience for city dwellers. Nowadays, only a dozen or so lidos remain, including Parliament Hill, Tooting Bec and Brockwell, though the recent reopening of Charlton and Hackney Lidos after decades of neglect may signal a renaissance. Long a popular swimming and sunbathing spot, the Serpentine got its own lido in 1931. Members of the Serpentine Swimming Club (founded 1864) take to the water every morning of the year, and the club's Christmas Day race (Santa hats optional) is a source of bemusement to tourists.

E Dean/Topical Press Agency/Hulton Archive

The Rolling Stones 1967

The 'greatest rock and roll band in the world' take a stroll in a London park. From left, Charlie Watts, Mick Jagger, Bill Wyman, Keith Richards and Brian Jones had, since 1962, found mega-stardom around the world as the Rolling Stones. Seen here at the time of the release of their album *Between the Buttons*, the band were entering a difficult period. Richards' home was raided the following month and he and Jagger were charged with drug offences. Richards said of the incident years later, 'When we got busted at Redlands, it suddenly made us realise that this was a whole different ball game and that was when the fun stopped. Up until then it had been as though London existed in a beautiful space where you could do anything you wanted.'

Keystone/Hulton Archive

Anti-apartheid protest 1985

A placard depicting South African president PW Botha is brandished at an anti-apartheid rally in Trafalgar Square. Such demonstrations were a regular feature of London life for decades, following the founding of the Anti-Apartheid Movement (originally the Boycott Movement) in 1959. Members of the AAM included the British Communist, Liberal and Labour Parties, as well as the TUC, the National Union of Students and some London churches. Prominent public figures included politicians Barbara Castle, Peter Hain and Frank Dobson as well as playwright Harold Pinter, actor Vanessa Redgrave and archbishop Trevor Huddleston. There was also a large group of African National Congress exiles in London, including ANC president Oliver Tambo. When Nelson Mandela was finally released from prison on 11 February 1990, the pavement outside Trafalgar Square's South Africa House – for years the site of protests by the AAM – became the scene of a joyous party.

Leon Morris/Hulton Archive

The Protein Man 1980

One of London's great eccentrics, Stanley Green was a familiar sight in the West End for decades. Every day for 25 years, from 1968 until his death in 1993, he paraded on Oxford Street carrying a placard that advised 'Less Passion from Less Protein'. Many passers-by ignored him, others were amused – and some even shelled out a few pence for a copy of his self-printed booklet, 'Eight Passion Proteins with Care'. Probably none, however, agreed with his belief that too much protein increased the sex drive to dangerous levels; Green's own diet consisted mainly of porridge, bread and barley water mixed with powdered milk. His notoriety won him a cameo in Ben Elton's novel *Gridlock*, a slot in the *Sunday Times*' 'A Life in the Day' column, and a mention in Peter Ackroyd's *London: A Biography*. Ackroyd wrote that Green 'was commonly ignored by the great tide of people who washed around him, and thus became a poignant symbol of the city's incuriosity and forgetfulness.' On Green's death, at the age of 78, the Museum of London acquired his placards and a set of his pamphlets.

Alan Davidson/Evening Standard/Hulton Archive

Window cleaning at Kew Gardens 1936

The huge task of cleaning the vast expanse of glass in the Palm and Temperate Houses in the Royal Botanical Gardens at Kew was undertaken annually with little more than ladders, mops and elbow grease. The Palm House, pictured here, was designed by architect Decimus Burton (a protégé of John Nash) and wrought-iron worker Richard Turner a few years after Kew officially became a national botanical garden in 1840 – at the time it was the largest greenhouse in the world. The ingenious design, modelled on ship-building methods (it's essentially an upside-down hull), allowed for the span and height necessary to give the tall palms imported from the tropics enough room to flourish.

Maeers/Fox Photos/Hulton Archive

Kindertransport 1939

Following the orgy of violence known as Kristallnacht on 9/10 November 1938, when Nazis in Germany and Austria burned and destroyed thousands of Jewish homes, businesses and synagogues, and incarcerated more than 30,000 Jewish men in concentration camps, Britain's refugee charities mobilised for action. Parliament agreed to admit an unspecified number of Jewish children up to the age of 17, and the Kindertransport operation was born. The first group of children left in December 1938, the last on 1 September 1939, two days before Britain entered the war. A total of around 10,000 children escaped from Austria, Germany, Poland and Czechoslovakia – this photo shows some of the 235 children who have just arrived at Liverpool Street station from Vienna in July 1939. Most children never saw their parents again.

George W Hales/Fox Photos/Hulton Archive

Tattersall's horse auction 1938

Every Monday from April 1865 until the outbreak of war in September 1939, the streets of Knightsbridge were filled with aristocrats and shady racecourse characters visiting one of the world's most famous horse auctioneers, Tattersall's. On two acres of land at Knightsbridge Green, 'Tatt's' traded everything from hunters and race horses to polo ponies and studs, displaying the bloodstock in the auction run, as seen here. Not everyone came to buy; two discreet and elegant rooms were betting shops, but the centrepiece of Tatt's was the auction yard, a huge galleried court covered by a soaring glass and iron roof and featuring the Fox, a drinking fountain in a classical stone cupola decorated with a stone fox and a bust of George IV. The former still stands in Tattersall's at Newmarket, overseeing the sale of 10,000 horses a year, all of them still priced in guineas.

Felix Man/Picture Post/Hulton Archive

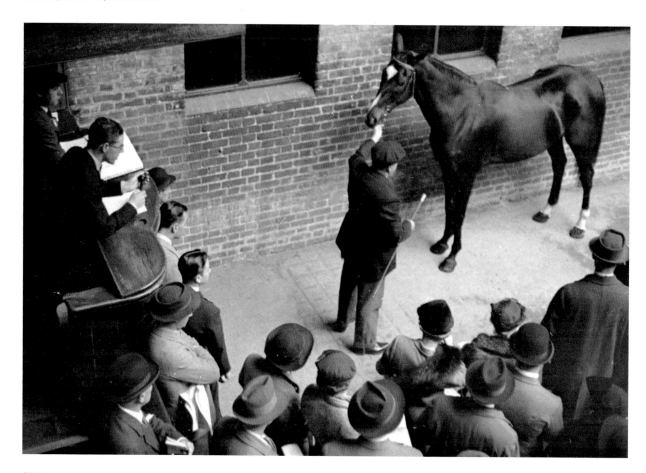

Crinolines on a bus 1854

More than 150 years ago, it was possible to catch a London bus that was manned by a uniformed conductor, carried more than 20 people comfortably, travelled at up to ten miles per hour, cost a shilling from Paddington to Bank, provided free newspapers and magazines – and could even accommodate a large number of ladies' crinolines. Such innovations were thanks to one George Shillibeer, who launched the capital's first horse-drawn omnibus on 4 July 1829. Rival omnibus companies swiftly sprang up; by 1842, competition between different outfits for passengers and journeys resulted in a driver being charged with manslaughter for running over a man in City Road while racing another bus. Fortunately for passers-by, no crinolines were involved.

London Stereoscopic Company/Hulton Archive

Eric Gill at Broadcasting House 1932

Sculptor, typographer, stonemason, writer, teacher and all-round eccentric, Eric Gill was one of the 20th century's most unconventional figures, his work both deeply religious and highly erotic – a direct echo of his private life, which included adultery, incest with his sister and his daughter, and sexual experiments with his dog (though little of this was known until revealed in a biography 40 years after his death). His best-known works include the carvings of Prospero and Ariel on the BBC's Broadcasting House in Langham Place – which he's working on here – the Stations of the Cross in Westminster Cathedral, and the much-used Gill Sans font, for years the typeface of Penguin Books paperbacks and British Railways.

Fox Photos/Hulton Archive

Anti-Italian riots 1940

Shopkeepers in Soho remove signs with the word 'Italian' from their premises after a wave of anti-Italian riots throughout the capital, following Mussolini's alliance with Hitler. Italian delis, restaurants and ice-cream parlours were attacked in other cities too, including Liverpool and Manchester. It wasn't just the mob's anger that Italian Londoners faced: Churchill ordered all Italian men aged 17 to 60 with less than 20 years' residence in the UK to be arrested. Many Italians living in Britain were interned; some had Nazi leanings, but others were left-wing opponents of Il Duce that had fled abroad after being involved in anti-fascist activities in Italy. Peppino Leoni, well-known owner of the famous Soho restaurant Quo Vadis, was incarcerated, despite having been in the UK since 1907.

Arthur Tanner/Fox Photos/Hulton Archive

Playing on the streets
1954

These pictures were taken for a *Picture Post* article entitled 'Children of the streets'. Nowadays, in an era of childhood obesity and parental panic, such scenes – kids playing on the capital's streets, with homemade toys and not a car or adult in sight – seem almost idyllic, but the article, by famous children's author Noel Streatfeild, was a condemnation not a celebration of life for London's youngsters. Bemoaning 'the problem of what to do with children, who, during the holidays, have nothing to do and nowhere to go', it demanded more public playgrounds and parks, and organised play schemes during the summer holidays.
Thurston Hopkins/Hulton Archive

Teddy bear shrubs 1945

'The useless but charming art of misleading nature up the garden path' is how the magazine *Picture Post* described topiary in September 1945, when this photograph of teddy bear-shaped shrubs appeared, alongside assorted birds, corkscrews and other fanciful creations. All were on display at Messrs Klinkert's Topiary Nurseries at Kew (regrettably, no longer in business). The art of clipping and training evergreens, mainly slow-growing box and yew, into specific shapes has a long and distinguished history, originating in Roman times and becoming fashionable again in the Middle Ages, Renaissance Italy and 17th-century France, notably at Versailles. London's public gardens aren't really known for their topiary (though Hampton Court has a few examples in addition to its famous maze): Levens Hall in Cumbria, the work of French designer Guillaume Beaumont, is the place to go for tip-top topiary.

Kurt Hutton/Hulton Archive

British Movement rally 1980

London's music scene in the late 1970s and early '80s was dominated by punk and its attendant left-wing and anti-racist ideology; the Anti-Nazi League and Rock Against Racism held huge demos and free concerts in the capital, as bands such as the Clash and the Specials developed styles that drew on ska, reggae and roots. A counter movement grew up at the same time: a young neo-fascist scene made up of white power skinheads from the National Front's Rock Against Communism and the British Movement, a neo-Nazi political party founded in 1968. BM members were proud of their violent behaviour, and vociferous in their encouragement of it at football matches and at rallies in racially mixed parts of town, such as here, in Notting Hill.
Stuart Nicol/Evening Standard/Hulton Archive

Empire Day 1913

Dressed head to toe in union flags, these children couldn't look more patriotic if they tried. Such scenes were a familiar sight up and down the land – and across the globe – for 50 years, as the British Empire's loyal subjects celebrated Empire Day on 24 May, Queen Victoria's birthday. The first Empire Day was held in 1902 (the year after Victoria's death), though it wasn't officially recognised until 1916. Rousing speeches, patriotic songs, flag-waving and dressing-up were the order of the day as schools, churches, villages and towns put on plays, pageants and exhibitions; the BBC broadcast special services and concerts, and the Daily Express Empire Festival was an annual fixture in Hyde Park into the '30s. The decline of empire made the event increasingly anachronistic, and in 1958 it was repackaged as the (largely ignored) Commonwealth Day.
Roper/Topical Press Agency/Hulton Archive

Hayward Gallery 1969

The external spaces of the South Bank have been loathed and loved in equal measure for the starkness of their Brutalist architecture. But the concrete severity has provided a wonderful backdrop to some unexpected and welcome humanising scenes. Among them have been weddings on the roof pavilions of the Royal Festival Hall, Antony Gormley's elegiac life-size cast-iron figures on the rooftops, an iconic impromptu skateboarding park on ground level – and this child playing with her dolls and bears outside the Hayward Gallery, a year after it opened, in one of the three spaces originally intended as outdoor sculpture courts.

Evening Standard/Hulton Archive

Wartime slogan 1940

A World War II hoarding exhorting Britain's workers, in the words of Herbert Morrison, home secretary and minister of home security, to 'Go to it!' Morrison's appeal in early June was part of the government's campaign to boost the country's industry and fortify civilian morale, particularly important when the German 'Blitzkrieg' was storming through Europe and the threat of invasion seemed very real. The message had an effect: many factories went to seven-day working, 12-hour shifts became commonplace and industrial disputes tailed off.

A Cook/London Express/Hulton Archive

New flooring for Carnaby Street 1973

Carnaby Street's fame began in the mid 1950s, when a shop called Vince opened on Newburgh Street, selling dandy clothes to celebrities. The area later became a vital part of the Mod scene, largely because of young menswear retailer John Stephens. By the mid '60s, it was a world-famous shopping street packed with one-off fashion boutiques, among them Lord John (and its female equivalent Lady Jane), Take Six, I Was Lord Kitchener's Valet and Gear. By the time this picture was taken, it was a shadow of its former glory as the centre of Swinging London – perhaps that's the reason Westminster Council decided to give the place a £60,000 facelift, which included installing this rubberised, coloured flooring (the street had recently been pedestrianised). A riot of beige and orange, it's as about as '70s as it comes.

Graham French/BIPs/Hulton Archive

Cricket coaching in Marylebone 1933

Who says women can't play cricket? Apparently, the female teacher (name not given) pictured here demonstrating a mean bowling action taught cricket at the London County Council's Oateforth School in Marylebone – with such success that her pupils, who had never played the game before, won the local schools junior cricket league at their first attempt. Such achievements shouldn't seem surprising: after all, women in Britain had been playing cricket since the 18th century, with the first all-women club formed in 1887 (in Yorkshire, of course). The nationwide Women's Cricket Association was set up in 1926 and – a year after this photograph was taken – the first women's Test match was played in Brisbane, between England and Australia. England won.

Fox Photos/Hulton Archive

Penny farthings at Herne Hill 1932

A group of elderly enthusiasts display their skill on penny farthings at the outdoor velodrome in Herne Hill. Track cycle racing was in its heyday in the 1920s and '30s, though the Victorian 'ordinary' (as the penny farthing was also known) had long fallen out favour by then. Although very stable at low speeds, it was a tricky contraption to ride with its five-foot-diameter front wheel, and was notoriously prone to accidents; a sudden stop meant the rider was likely to be catapulted over the handlebars. Built in 1891, the Herne Hill velodrome is the sole survivor of the numerous Victorian cycling tracks that once dotted the capital. It was used for the 1948 London Olympics and its Good Friday meetings (first held in 1903) still draw massive crowds.

Douglas Miller/Topical Press Agency/Hulton Archive

Art on the South Bank 1951

The visual arts were a major feature of the 1951 Festival of Britain, with paintings, sculptures, murals and films shown in touring exhibitions or decorating the various festival pavilions. Specially commissioned works by the great and the good of the British art world, including Henry Moore, Jacob Epstein, Barbara Hepworth, Eduardo Paolozzi and Lynn Chadwick, were dotted about the main South Bank site – most were temporary creations that lasted only as long as the festival itself. One of the most prominent pieces was *The Islanders* (left), a monumental stone relief of three figures by Viennese émigré Siegfried Charoux, while one of the most praised was Victor Pasmore's massive abstract mural, *The Waterfall* (far left). Here, Pasmore is painting the black and white spiral design on to ceramic tiles, which were then fixed to the exterior of the Regatta Restaurant.

Charles Hewitt/Hulton Archive

Barges in the Pool of London 1900

With the new Tower Bridge (opened in 1894) in the distance, barges loaded with everything from cinnamon to coffee and wool to marble are stacked up against one another waiting to transport their cargoes up and down the river. The Pool of London, the area between London Bridge and Rotherhithe, was of crucial importance to the capital for centuries; in fact, it was the very reason for London's long role as the world's leading port. Following the expansion of the British Empire in the 18th and 19th centuries, the wharves lining both sides of the Thames became so crowded with traffic that it was said you could cross from one side of the river to the other simply by stepping from boat to boat.
Roger Viollet

Hunting on Oxford Street 1926

It's hard to work out why this group of horses and hounds, plus assorted schoolboys, should be hanging around Oxford Circus, but perhaps they're on their way to Soho. It would be appropriate (if still strange), as the area was once Henry VII's royal hunting ground and derives its name from the ancient hunting cry of 'So-ho'. Or perhaps it was an early if misguided attempt to deal with the problem of urban foxes.

Fox Photos/Hulton Archive

London Ski-Jumping Contest 1950

One of the bizarrest sights to have graced Hampstead Heath, this 62-foot-high ramp was erected on a hill next to the Vale of Health for the London Ski-Jumping Contest on 25 March 1950. Twenty-five Norwegian skiers came over for the event, organised by the Central Council of Physical Recreation in association with the Ski Club of Great Britain and Oslo Ski Club. The Scandinavians brought with them – packed in wooden boxes and insulated with dry ice – the 45 tons of snow used to cover the slope. The ramp provided jumpers with a 100-foot run-up, marginally shorter than a full-size jump. Vast crowds flocked to the Heath to see the event, and a commentator was on hand to explain the finer points of each jump. Oxford defeated Cambridge in the University Challenge Cup, and an all-comers' contest, the London Challenge Cup, was won, not surprisingly, by a Norwegian, Arne Hoel. Despite is popularity, the ski-jump competition never took place again.

Fred Morley/Fox Photos/Hulton Archive

Kingsway Subway 1952

At the junction of Southampton Row and Vernon Place in Holborn, behind a padlocked gate, a strange set of tracks lead down a cobbled road to the darkness of a disappearing tunnel. These are the tram tracks that lead to the disused Kingsway Subway and its two stations, Holborn and Aldwych. From 1906 to 1930, single-deck electric trams ran between Angel Islington and Aldwych: the journey took 12 minutes northbound, ten southbound. Double-decker trams came later, but only the 31, 33 and 35, the 'Kingsway Routes', survived the war, lasting until 1952. Since then, the subway has been used to house back-up buses for the coronation, as an underpass for traffic coming off Waterloo Bridge (a function it still serves today), as a film location, a gallery and a dead road signs storage depot for Camden Council.

Topical Press Agency/Hulton Archive

East End family 1912

Britain was in the midst of political reform in the early 20th century as the Liberal party edged towards socialism and the Prime Minister, David Lloyd George, ushered in the beginnings of a basic welfare state, but free healthcare, education and a social support system were still a long way off in 1912 – which might explain why the father of this impoverished East End family displays a handful of pawn tickets for the photographer.
Topical Press Agency/Hulton Archive

Caribbean immigrants 1956

Haywood Magee's photo of West Indian immigrants at Victoria Station, fresh from Southampton docks, didn't actually appear in the *Picture Post* article for which it was taken – though it's been published frequently since. The arrival of 500 West Indians on the SS *Empire Windrush* in 1948 marks the beginning of mass emigration from the Caribbean, which really took off in the 1950s. Escaping high unemployment and drawn by Britain's post-war labour shortage and the 1948 Nationality Act (which bestowed citizenship rights on members of the Commonwealth), around 177,000 West Indians had reached the UK by 1961. The vast majority settled in the capital, many finding jobs with London Transport and the National Health Service.

Haywood Magee/Hulton Archive

Ruins of the Crystal Palace 1936

The glass-and-iron Crystal Palace was built in Hyde Park in 1851 to house the Great Exhibition; six years later it was moved to Sydenham where it stood until consumed by fire on 30 November 1936. The conflagration was the most spectacular seen in Britain for many years. It spread with such rapidity that within half an hour the whole building was ablaze; around 90 engines, 500 fireman and 750 policemen were engaged in fighting the flames. Only the two massive north and south towers (one is visible in the background) escaped destruction, though they were taken down in 1941 because, at 282 feet, they were a conspicuous landmark for enemy bombers.
Popperfoto

The Beatles on stage 1963

Mop-topped, smartly dressed and ridiculously fresh-faced, the Beatles rehearse for the Royal Variety Performance to be held later that night, 4 November, at London's Prince of Wales Theatre. It was just a couple of weeks before the release of the Fab Four's second album, *With the Beatles*, and Beatlemania had reached fever pitch in the UK. Although only seventh on a bill of 19 and playing just four songs, the band stole the show (much to the annoyance of the top-billed Marlene Dietrich), with Lennon famously quipping to the audience as he introduced 'Twist & Shout': 'Will the people in the cheaper seats clap their hands? And the rest of you – if you'll just rattle your jewellery.'

Central Press/Hulton Archive

Playing football with a panda 1959

London Zoo's female panda, Chi Chi, plays keepy-uppy with her keeper, Alan Kent. Chi Chi had arrived a year earlier, and instantly became the zoo's most popular exhibit – a position she held until her death in 1972. She was the only giant panda in the west, and was also the inspiration for the World Wildlife Fund's symbol. Chi Chi was originally intended for Washington Zoo, but Cold War animosity had led the US government to ban all trade with Communist China; as 'communist goods' she was refused entry to the US. Although the Zoological Society of London was against the collection of wild pandas, it accepted Chi Chi as she'd already been captured. Chi Chi can still be seen: stuffed, she sits in a display case in the café at the Natural History Museum.

Fox Photos/Hulton Archive

Hampstead women's pond 1935

Hardy swimmers are undeterred by a frozen December day at the women's pond on Hampstead Heath. Officially the Kenwood Ladies' Bathing Pond, it's the newest of the Heath's three freshwater swimming pools, opened in 1925; the men's pond (the biggest) has been in use since the 1890s and the mixed pond since the 1860s. Originally dug as reservoirs in the 17th century, and fed by the River Fleet, they are used by more than 200,000 people each year, though few brave the murky waters in winter. Threats by the Corporation of London, which manages the Heath, to close the ponds on cost grounds in 2004 were met with uproar and headlines in the national press.

E Dean/Topical Press Agency/Hulton Archive

SS Great Eastern 1857

The great Victorian engineer Isambard Kingdom Brunel's final work, the massive iron steamship the *Great Eastern* – seen here nearing completion in a dry dock at Millwall – was a doomed vessel. Financial and technical difficulties plagued the project, several workers were killed during construction and Brunel himself suffered a stroke and died shortly after her maiden voyage. Instead of becoming the world's greatest passenger ship, as Brunel had intended, she ended up laying transatlantic cables before being broken up for scrap. Photographer Robert Howlett, who had been commissioned by the *Illustrated Times* to document the building of the ship, also died shortly after her launch in 1858, aged 27 – supposedly poisoned by his own photographic chemicals. He also took the famous portrait of Brunel standing with top hat and cigar in front of the ship's massive chains.

Robert Howlett/George Eastman House/Hulton Archive

Fluffers in the Underground 1952

Long before the name became synonymous with the porn industry, fluffers, or fluffies, were hard at work deep in London's tube network, using brushes and brooms to clean the tunnels at night once the last trains had run. The work continues today, and Molly Dineen's 1989 documentary *The Heart of the Angel*, shot at Angel tube station, gives a telling insight into just how little such jobs have changed in 50 years, the women stripping down to don overalls on the deserted station platforms before heading into the dark to perform their tasks.

Topical Press Agency/Hulton Archive

Liverpool Street station 1900

A railway worker adjusts the clock at Liverpool Street station for daylight saving time. The year is unspecified, but it's around the start of the 20th century – about 25 years after the station had opened, built on the former site of the Bethlem Royal Hospital (aka Bedlam, the notorious lunatic asylum). The steam locomotives have long gone, of course, British Rail's last passenger steam train puffing into oblivion in 1968. The station is also unrecognisable, having been extensively remodelled in the 1980s and '90s, although the slender cast-iron columns topped with acanthus leaves and delicate tracery (just visible in the background) remain.

FPG/Hulton Archive

Barbara Hepworth at the Tate
1965

World-renowned sculptor Barbara Hepworth peers through the hole in her marble work, *Pierced Form*, at the Tate Gallery. She had presented the sculpture to the gallery the year before. The Tate still owns the piece, as well as nearly 130 other Hepworth sculptures – many on show at her former house and studio in St Ives, Cornwall (where she died in a fire in 1975). For Londoners, the easiest place to see a Hepworth is on Oxford Street, where her cast-aluminium piece *Winged Figure* has graced the exterior of department store John Lewis for 45 years.

Central Press/Hulton Archive

Street parties 1918, 1953

Historically, street parties are the time-honoured way for Londoners to celebrate momentous public events, with cakes, bunting and smartly dressed children turning out for such occasions as the end of World War I (below) and the coronation in 1953 (right). Such parties are less common nowadays, though there was a revival of sorts for the Queen's Silver Jubilee in 1977. The coronation celebrations on Morpeth Street, Hackney, were recorded by Thurston Hopkins and John Chillingworth, two of *Picture Post*'s star photographers, for an article entitled 'Cockneys' Own Party'. Local residents raised £163 for the big day, prompting the magazine to observe: 'Cockneys don't read history – they live it.'

Central Press/Hulton Archive

Thurston Hopkins/Picture Post/Hulton Archive

Michael Caine 1965

Born Maurice Joseph Micklewhite in Rotherhithe, Michael Caine was 32 when this picture was taken. Having been a bit-part actor for about ten years, by 1965 Caine was rising to prominence after starring in *Zulu* and as Harry Palmer in *The Ipcress File*. The following year he become a household name playing the title role in *Alfie*. Not only does Caine have the distinction of being one of only two actors (the other is Jack Nicholson) to have been nominated for an Oscar every decade since the 1960s, but his iconic status is confirmed by the fact that in the last ten years there have been remakes of four of the films he originally starred in: *Alfie*, *Get Carter*, *The Italian Job* and *Sleuth*. Not a lot of people know that...
Stephan C Archetti/Hulton Archive

Squatters at Centre Point 1973

Possessing an 'elegance worthy of a Wren steeple', according to the Royal Fine Art Commission, and considered 'coarse in the extreme' by critic Nikolaus Pevsner, the perennially controversial Centre Point was one of London's first skyscrapers. It was designed by Richard Seifert (also behind the NatWest Tower) and completed in 1966. Its 32 floors remained empty for over a decade as millionaire property speculator and developer Harry Hyams waited for a single tenant to occupy the whole building – and watched the rent rate soar. The absurdity of this situation was not lost on architecture students keen to see more residential housing in the city and who protested by squatting in the building in 1973. Campaigners fighting homelessness occupied the building the following year and then went on to found the housing charity Centrepoint.
Stroud/Express/Hulton Archive

Football World Cup 1966

To make sure that no one got lost on the way to Wembley Stadium, the Automobile Association put up 1,400 new road signs in London before the 1966 World Cup, hosted by England. Wembley wasn't the only ground used during the tournament, of course, but it was the venue for the controversial, nail-biting final on 30 July, where England beat West Germany 4-2 in extra time. Geoff Hurst played himself into the history books by becoming the first (and only) player to score a hat trick in a World Cup Final. Over 96,000 spectators packed the stadium and another 400 million around the world watched the match on television.

Popperfoto

Policeman herding sheep 1931

This impressive flock of sheep is being moved from Hyde Park to Green Park under the watchful eye of a smartly dressed bobby. Until 1935 sheep and cattle grazed regularly on London's open land, heaths, commons and parks, before ending up at livestock markets such as Smithfields, and the sight of a flock being herded down a major thoroughfare such as Kingsway, holding up the traffic at Aldwych or strolling across Waterloo Bridge was a relatively common sight.

Fox Photos/Hulton Archive

Petal eyelashes
1969

Cosmetics fashions come and go as they have done since the days of sooty kohls in Ancient Egypt and the lead-based foundations used in the 16th century. But the false eyelash indisputably belongs to the decade of the 1960s. Eylure, a pioneer in false lash technology, had been in the business of providing professional make-up to film stars since the 1940s, but by the '60s demand on the high street was so intense – thanks in large part to Mary Quant – that the firm went mainstream and opened a shop in Grosvenor Street. By 1969 the trend had reached its zenith: these beauties, made from fake flower petals and real hair, cost five guineas a pair.

Keystone/Hulton Archive

Soho's Windmill Theatre 1964

Three showgirls sit glumly in the café of the Windmill Theatre after hearing that the building is about to be turned into a cinema, its long-running *Revudeville* show unable to compete with the growing number of strip joints and massage parlours in Soho. The variety show, playing non-stop six days a week, opened in 1932, shocking and delighting Londoners in equal measure with its singers, dancers, comedians and – especially – glamorous female nudes, who got round the obscenity laws by posing motionless: 'if it moves, it's rude'. Patrons would make an unseemly scramble for the first row to get the best view of the girls, the so-called 'Windmill Steeplechase'. The theatre was also famous for staying open throughout the war, apart from the compulsory 12-day shutdown of all West End theatres in September 1939.

Keystone/Hulton Archive

Iraq war demonstration 2003

London has seen innumerable protests, marches and demonstrations in support of all sorts of causes during its long history, but the biggest of them all – the biggest in the country, in fact – was on 15 February 2003, a month before the US-led invasion of Iraq. Estimates of the number of people who turned out that day vary, inevitably, depending on who's doing the counting: figures range from 750,000 (according to the police) to around two million (according to the Stop the War Coalition, which organised the event). Whatever the correct tally, the peace protest was a massive and unprecedented display of public feeling – as this picture taken at the end of the march, in Hyde Park, makes clear.
Scott Barbour

Flooding in the Mall
1934

We don't know who this young man is or why he's stepping so elegantly across a flooded stretch of the Mall with the aid of two chairs and an umbrella, but it certainly makes an appealing photograph. The Mall – possibly the grandest street in London, and the only one that really deserves to be called a boulevard – was created out of St James's Park in 1660 as a pitch for *paille-maille* (a croquet-like game popular at the time), lined by two avenues of trees in the French fashion. Nearby Pall Mall was also used for the same purpose, hence its name.

HF Davis/Hulton Archive

Moving Eros 1925

One of the capital's most famous statues arrived in Piccadilly Circus in 1893 atop a fountain erected in honour of the renowned Victorian philanthropist the Earl of Shaftesbury. The winged nude has been there ever since, apart from the occasional cleaning and during World War II, when he was removed for safe-keeping and the fountain covered in advertising hoardings. Intended by sculptor Alfred Gilbert to depict Anteros, the god of requited love, the statue is also called 'The Angel of Christian Charity', but most know him as Eros, the god of erotic love – which seems the most fitting choice, considering Soho's long connection with the sex industry.

E Bacon/Topical Press Agency/Hulton Archive

The General Strike 1926

Children with empty sacks wait hopefully for lumps of coal to fall from vans at the coal yards at King's Cross during the General Strike. Triggered by threatened wage cuts to coal miners, the strike began on 3 May, with railway and transport workers, printers, dockers and iron and steel workers joining the picket. The following day in London, only 15 out of 315 tubes, 300 out of 4,400 buses and nine out of 2,000 trams operated. The government had been expecting a strike for nine months so there were reserves of essential supplies and army was used to provide services. The TUC called off the strike after nine days; the miners stuck it out for another six months, but were eventually forced back to work, having gained nothing. Many lost their jobs, and those that didn't had to accept longer hours and lower wages.

HF Davis/Topical Press Agency/Hulton Archive

Keystone Features/Hulton Archive

London's original Chinatown 1927

Limehouse was the centre of London's first Chinatown, formed in the 1880s by an enclave of Cantonese sailors. Chinese cafés, grocers and laundries grew up around Pennyfields and Limehouse Causeway. The area developed an unsavoury reputation, largely because of (legal) opium smoking, and the penny press stoked up fears of the 'Yellow Peril' – an atmosphere exacerbated by novelists such as Sax Rohmer, creator of Fu Manchu; Oscar Wilde's Dorian Gray came to Limehouse to buy opium, as did Sherlock Holmes. Xenophobic riots in 1919 were followed by clearances of the Chinese 'slums' in the 1930s. The area was further decimated by the Blitz, and most of the remaining residents moved to the streets south of Soho. Nowadays, apart from some street names – Nankin, Canton, Pekin, Mandarin – few traces of its Eastern heritage remain.

Boats in Battersea Park 1939

Head boatman Mr Stokes gives his craft a final check before the start of the Easter boating season. Battersea is by no means the only London park where nautical types can take to the water, but the size of the boating lake, its squiggly layout and leafy surroundings makes a voyage here an almost rural experience. The 200 acres of riverside land were once marshy fields – where the Duke of Wellington, when prime minister, famously fought a duel with the Earl of Winchilsea – and then used for market gardening. Opened in 1858, the park (and lake) were part of a wave of Victorian schemes intended to promote public health among the capital's fast-expanding population.

Harry Todd/Fox Photos/Hulton Archive

Battersea Dogs Home 1980

A soulful-looking bassett hound poses in a kennel at Battersea Dogs & Cats Home for a picture that was used in a pre-Christmas advertising campaign to help find owners for the thousands of strays that the organisation takes in each year. With the aim of never turning away a dog or cat in need, the famous pet charity was the first of its kind in the UK, founded in 1860 by Mary Tealby. Originally based in Holloway, in 1871 it moved to its current headquarters in Battersea. Perhaps surprisingly, the centre's workload was greatest in the 1890s, when it received about four times as many animals as in the 1990s.

Michael Fresco/Evening Standard/Hulton Archive

Teddy boy at Elephant & Castle 1955

The original teenagers, the Teddy boys got their name from the Edwardian-style suits they sported after World War II. A subculture that was born in a booming London – and for the first time identified its newly financially independent members as neither children nor adults – Teddies also strongly associated themselves with the new rock 'n' roll music coming out of the States in the 1950s. It is perhaps no coincidence that there is something strikingly James Dean-like about this image. (The film star died a couple of months after the picture was taken.)
Popperfoto

Listening booths 1955

The post-war years saw a huge boom in the sale of records, with two new formats coming on the market at the end of the 1940s: the 12-inch, 33rpm LP (for 'long play') and the seven-inch, 45rpm single. Here, ranks of customers try before they buy in the sound-proofed listening booths that used to fill music shops in the days before headphones became ubiquitous. Vinyl dominated the audio business for most of the 20th century, and each booth would have its own gramophone attached. Those were the days.

John Drysdale/Keystone/Hulton Archive

Solar eclipse 1927

Hysteria gripped the nation in advance of the total solar eclipse of 29 June 1927 as the next one to be visible from the UK mainland wasn't due for another 72 years, until 11 August 1999. The track of totality was narrow, covering a 42-mile band from North Wales to Hartlepool, and the eclipse itself lasted only 23 seconds, but for weeks beforehand children throughout Britain had lessons on solar science, wrote special projects and practised safe viewing methods, such as using two photographic negatives sandwiched together, as in this north London school. Thousands travelled across the country to view the phenomenon, but most were disappointed as heavy rain obscured the spectacle – though, fortunately, the clouds cleared in Giggleswick, Yorkshire, where the Royal Observatory had sent an eclipse expedition.

Kirby/Topical Press Agency/Hulton Archive

R101 airship 1929

The giant airship R101 flies over St Paul's Cathedral during a test flight. The pride of Britain's burgeoning aviation industry, she was the biggest dirigible in the world at the time: 777 feet long, with a volume of 5.5 million cubic feet – slightly larger than her arch rival, the famous German airship Graf Zeppelin. The luxurious interiors featured two levels of passenger accommodation, including promenade areas with deckchairs, a 60-seat dining room and even a smoking room. A year later, the R101 set off for Karachi in India on her first major flight, but a combination of gusting winds and the inherently unstable design resulted in the airship crashing into a hillside near Beauvais, just north of Paris. The leaking hydrogen exploded, fire engulfed the whole structure and within seconds she was a skeleton of twisted metal. Forty-six of the 54 passengers and crew were killed.

Topical Press Agency/Hulton Archive

Coronations 1937, 1953

These near-identical photographs – taken from almost the same spot on the edge of Trafalgar Square, with Admiralty Arch in the top left – are of the coronations of King George VI, on 12 May 1937 (left), and Queen Elizabeth II, on 2 June 1953. The processions are heading in opposite directions, but otherwise the scenes are very similar: grey and rainy weather, miles of ceremonial bunting, huge crowds. Both events were televised: George VI's coronation procession was the first outside broadcast for the BBC's recently launched television service, viewed by a paltry 10,000 people, while over 20 million worldwide tuned in for his daughter's investiture 16 years later. For many it was their first experience of the wonders of television (black and white, of course) and marked the arrival of TV as a mass medium.

Popperfoto

Fleet sewer 1914

Sewer workers have always needed a strong light, and a stronger stomach, when examining the 30,000 miles of underground tunnels that snake throughout the metropolis – including the culverts of the Fleet sewer, seen here, which make use of London's famous 'lost' River Fleet. The 82 miles of elegant brick tunnels are still explored on rare tours by amateur enthusiasts. They run the risk of diseases like hepatitis and rabies, and have come across some unexpected sights: horses' bodies, a hand grenade, prams, goldfish, FOG (fat, oil and grease) and cotton buds – the bane of the modern sewerage system for their unique ability to perfectly clog the 6mm holes of the sieving drums at Abbey Mills.

George Konig/Keystone/Hulton Archive

Fighting polar bears 1967

London Zoo's polar bears have always been star attractions. Celebrity inmates over the years have included Brumas, a female born in 1949 and the first polar bear to be successfully reared in Britain, and Pipaluk, a male born in 1967 to the bears pictured here. Sam (left) and Sally, named after the zoo's then bear keeper and his fiancée, arrived as cubs from Moscow Zoo and had three offspring together. But mating 700lb animals is not an easy business and Sally was mauled to death by Sam in 1975 after she spurned his advances. Polar bears disappeared from the zoo in 1985, when the Mappin Terraces, where all the bears were housed, were closed.

Evening Standard/Hulton Archive

Whippet racing in Custom House 1927

Hurling your prized dog into a race by its ears and tail was the traditional way of getting things going in a whippet race. In the 19th century, keeping a whippet – 'the poor man's racehorse' – was an enormously popular pastime, even more so than football, and wasn't confined to the north of England. On their days off, men would pit their dogs against others in fields and on city roads. Known as 'rag races', these typically took place on straight 200-yard tracks, using a piece of cloth as a lure, with dogs reaching speeds of up to 30mph. 'Snap-dog coursing' was another common, if cruel, event. Participants would place their whippets in an enclosure containing rabbits or rats and bet on which dog would snap up the most.

Fox Photos/Hulton Archive

Guinness poster 1952

Of all the acclaimed adverts for Guinness over the years, the animals in the 'My Goodness, My Guinness' campaign that appeared from the 1930s to the '60s were some of the most popular. Artist John Gilroy, of leading ad agency SH Benson, was the artist responsible for bringing the menagerie to life; a lion, kangaroo, gnu, pelican, ostrich, sea lion, tortoise, toucan and – here, an upside-down kinkajou – were among the animals featured, all stealing a pint of Guinness from a harassed zoo keeper. Gilroy's connection with the brand was long-lasting; he produced innumerable press ads and nearly 50 posters over 35 years, including the well-known image of a man casually carrying a girder under the 'Guinness for strength' slogan.

Davis/Picture Post/Hulton Archive

Mosley inspects his Blackshirts 1936

Sir Oswald Mosley salutes his followers at a parade on Royal Mint Street – just hours before the Battle of Cable Street, a key event in Britain's anti-fascist history. Vain, charismatic and a mesmerising orator, Mosley founded the British Union of Fascists in 1932, having tried and rejected the Conservative, Liberal and Labour parties. Earlier in 1936, he had married celebrated beauty Diana Mitford, one of the famous Mitford sisters, in a secret wedding at the Berlin home of Nazi propaganda chief Joseph Goebbels; Hitler was one of the guests. The Mosleys were interned for much of the war in a house in the grounds of Holloway Prison; there were large-scale protests when they were released in 1943. Mosley died in 1980, his wife in 2003.

Central Press/Hulton Archive

Battle of Cable Street 1936

A crowd of anti-fascist demonstrators flees as police break down a barricade in Cable Street, Whitechapel, on Sunday 4 October 1936. The police were overseeing a proposed march through the working-class and heavily Jewish area by Oswald Mosley and his British Union of Fascists; thousands of demonstrators, a mix of communists, socialists, Jews, trade unionists, Irish dockers and East Enders, were attempting to stop them. They set up roadblocks with paving stones, furniture and overturned lorries while shouting the Spanish Civil War cry of *No pasaran* ('They shall not pass'). After a series of running battles, the march was abandoned and Mosley's Blackshirts dispersed. Subsequently, the Public Order Act was passed, banning political uniforms and requiring police consent for political marches. A huge mural on Cable Street commemorates the incident, as does a red plaque in Dock Street.

David Savill/Topical Press Agency/Hulton Archive

View across the Thames 1904

This atmospheric shot across the Thames of industrial buildings in Wapping, with a solitary ferryman in the foreground, is typical of the 'pictorialist' approach by American-born British photographer Alvin Langdon Coburn. He was a leading light in Alfred Stieglitz's Photo-Secession group, which favoured labour-intensive printing processes and championed photography as an art form rather than merely a mechanical method of reproduction; many of Coburn's pictures were published in Stieglitz's showcase magazine *Camera Work*. He created some memorable images of New York's Flatiron Building and aerial shots of Madison Square Park, as well as later portraits of such luminaries as WB Yeats, George Bernard Shaw, Henry James, Auguste Rodin and Henri Matisse.

Alvin Langdon Coburn/George Eastman House/ Hulton Archive

New Victoria cinema 1930

Opened in 1930, the New Victoria (now called the Apollo Victoria) is still the West End's largest theatre and, for an astounding 18 years, played host to Andrew Lloyd Webber's roller-musical *Starlight Express*. An art deco splendour, the theatre (originally used as a cinema and variety venue) was built with identical east and west facades for Provincial Cinematograph Theatres by architects Ernest Wainsley Lewis and William Edward Trent, who designed over 20 cinemas throughout Britain from the 1910s to the '30s. The chattering-class comedy *On Approval* (1927) – showing here in its first film version – was one of dramatist Frederick Lonsdale's biggest hits.

Sasha/Hulton Archive

Smoking at Wimbledon 1938

American Helen Jacobs lights up while Bill Tilden (centre) and Bunny Austin look on. Although Jacobs reached the finals of Wimbledon six times, she won just once, in 1936. Tilden (nicknamed 'Big Bill' on account of his gangly frame) was the first American to win the men's championship, in 1920 and 1921. He was also the oldest when he won for a third time in the 1930 at the age of 37. In 1950 he was voted the greatest tennis player of the first half of the 20th century in an Associated Press poll (shortly after being released from prison, for the second time, for making unwanted advances to a teenage boy). South Londoner Austin, meanwhile, remains the last British male player to have reached a Wimbledon singles final, in 1938.

Hudson/Topical Press Agency/Hulton Archive

Making a ghost 1965

An employee of Gems Wax Models conjures a fibreglass spirit in the company's factory in Notting Hill. Lit from the inside, the model was destined for the Mission San Juan Capistrano in Orange County, California, where it was to represent a ghost that scared a Native American novice to death. Founded in 1885, Gems specialised in making tailors' models for the European aristocracy, later adding heads and hands to the torsos to produce some of the earliest shop mannequins and models for the burgeoning museum industry. In the 1930s, it moved into the world of animatronics. Now situated in Park Royal and called Gems Display Models, it's the largest commercial wax sculptor in the world. Its work is displayed in venues across London, including the Imperial War Museum, the Sherlock Holmes Museum, Kensington Palace and RAF Hendon.

Chris Ware/Keystone/Hulton Archive

Cleaning an ichthyosaur 1930

The 29 prehistoric monsters of Crystal Palace Park unveiled in 1854 were the first ever models of dinosaurs, and were created four years before anyone had found a complete dinosaur skeleton. Consequently, they are now agreed to be largely inaccurate, though at the time they caused uproar in their contravention of widely held theological beliefs. The sculptures were made, in concrete, by Benjamin Waterhouse Hawkins, working closely with leading palaeontologist of the day Professor Richard Owen, the man who coined the term dinosaur (literally 'terrible lizard'). After extensive refurbishment, the sculptures were given Grade I listed status in 2007.

Fox Photos/Hulton Archive

Bugatti Aerolithe 1935

Appearing for the first time in public at the London and Paris Motor Shows in 1935 was one of the automobile world's most prized and rarest cars. The 3.3-litre Bugatti Type 57S Aerolithe coupe was an instant sensation – for its lightweight construction, 123mph top speed and, especially, its curvacious teardrop body, a triumph of art moderne styling. The vehicle was made, unusually, of electron, an alloy of magnesium and aluminium that is very light but can't be welded because it's also highly flammable – hence the rivets (visible on the left-hand fin). The riveting was kept on the production version even though it wasn't necessary as it was built from aluminium. Only four cars were ever made, all called the Atlantic; of these only two survive, one owned by fashion designer Ralph Lauren.

Topical Press Agency/Hulton Archive

Football match at Highbury 1956

A capacity crowd of around 51,000 watch Arsenal's first game of the season in 1956. Like the club itself, the stadium at Highbury went through numerous ups and downs during its 93-year history. Opened in 1913, it was given a splendid art deco overhaul in the 1930s, but was bombed during the war, the roof on the north terrace only being replaced in the year this picture was taken. Highbury also caused controversy in the hooligan years of the 1980s by refusing to install perimeter fencing, a move that saw it struck off the list of suitable FA Cup semi-final venues. Following more renovations to comply with seating regulations in the '90s, it closed in 2006, replaced by the shiny new Emirates stadium in Holloway; the old building has been turned into an upmarket apartment complex, and the pitch replaced by a communal garden.

Popperfoto

Martin Luther King 1964

In December 1964, Martin Luther King stopped off in London en route to Oslo to collect the Nobel Peace Prize, and was photographed in Embankment Gardens with Ralph Abernathy, his number two in the civil rights movement. King stayed at the Hilton, spoke at St Paul's Cathedral and visited Parliament. Four years later, King was assassinated while standing on a motel balcony in Memphis; his killer, James Earl Ray, fled the States and was finally arrested at Heathrow Airport. King now has a permanent presence in London, in the shape of a statue above the Great West Door of Westminster Abbey.

Reg Lancaster/Express/Hulton Archive

Skateboarder on the South Bank 2000

The undercroft beneath the Queen Elizabeth Hall on the South Bank has been a mecca for skateboarders since the 1970s, when the sport first took off in Britain. Generations of skaters (and BMXers) have learned tricks and taken tumbles while navigating the area's stairs, banks, ramps and railings, to the sometime annoyance of the authorities and the amusement of Londoners and visitors. Whether skaters will be practising and perfoming here in the future remains uncertain. As the redevelopment of the South Bank continues, there are rumours that the space will be turned into commercial units and the boarders relocated – but no purpose-built skate park could replicate the organic vibrancy of the original.
Ian Walton

Britons to Brisbane 1957

In the years after the war, Australia desperately needed labour, and many Europeans desperately needed a new start. The Rivetts from Walworth – including brothers Richard, Peter and Jim, seen here – were just one family who answered the New World's call, which had begun ten years earlier with an emigration wave that saw nearly 200,000 people leave Europe for Australia by 1950. A million more would arrive in each of the following four decades. The Rivett family was part of the new 'Bring out a Briton' campaign, which focused on the receiving Australian community rather than the migrants, encouraging them to sponsor individual families and help them settle in their new life.

Rand/Express/Hulton Archive

A falling fireman 1922

As colleagues hold a taut safety blanket, a fireman demonstrates the most effective technique for emergency defenestration at the London Fire Brigade's old headquarters on Southwark Bridge Road. The capital's fire service has a venerable history dating back to 1833, and its HQ has relocated a few times since then. As of early 2008 it is just round the corner from the original on Union Street, and the building pictured here has been put to use as the London Fire Brigade Museum.

Topical Press Agency/Hulton Archive

Crowd in Lambeth
1938

'A policeman's lot is not a happy one,' trilled Gilbert & Sullivan and it was certainly a hard life being a copper in London in the 1930s. There were fascist demonstrations, striking workers and IRA bombs to contend with, as well as the everyday chores of walking the beat, keeping the peace and telling the time. But worst of all was having to deal with a mob of tearful, excited children, desperate to catch a glimpse of Queen Mary, who was visiting Lambeth to open an extension to the town hall.

Topical Press Agency/Hulton Archive

Bus on a boat 1966

Along with Nelson's Column and the black cab, the Routemaster has been an instantly recognisable symbol of London for decades. So much so that in 1966 two buses were loaded – with some difficulty – on to a boat at Millwall Dock to be transported to Oslo, where they carried visitors to and from the 'British Fortnight' trade fair. The first Routemaster was built in the early '50s, though the standard 72-seat RML model didn't appear until 1961. Designed specifically for the capital's streets, it was a revolutionary vehicle for its day, with an aluminium body, automatic gearbox, power steering, advanced suspension system and hop-on, hop-off rear platform.

Keystone/Hulton Archive

Beat poets at the Albert Hall 1965

Mayhem, marijuana and some mind-blowing poetry are what characterised the International Poetry Incarnation at the Royal Albert Hall on 11 June 1965. Seven thousand people turned up for the hastily arranged event to hear readings and rants by American Beat poets Allen Ginsberg (centre, bearded), Lawrence Ferlinghetti and Gregory Corso and their UK counterparts, including Adrian Mitchell, Christopher Logue, Michael Horovitz, Spike Hawkins and Alexander Trocchi (on Ginsberg's right). Guitarist Davy Graham joined in, flowers were strewn about the stage and, inevitably, some people got naked. Billed as Britain's first 'happening', it was a formative event for the burgeoning counter-culture movement, captured memorably in Peter Whitehead's film *Wholly Communion*.

Michael Stroud/Express/Hulton Archive

Victorian street scenes 1877

One of the earliest examples of photography as social documentary, *Street Life in London* was published in 1877 by the pioneering Scottish photographer John Thomson and the union activist and journalist Adolphe Smith. It's still in print. Lengthy descriptions accompany each photo of the various people who scraped a living on the capital's streets, including cabbies, doctors, chimney sweeps, Romanies, barrow boys, musicians, ice-cream sellers and Covent Garden flower women. Above is a 'dealer in fancy-ware', one of the 1,500 or so traders selling cheap jewellery and ornaments from streetside barrows and stalls. Probably the most harrowing subject is this homeless woman minding a baby (right), one of the 'Crawlers of St Giles's' – described by Smith as the 'wrecks of humanity' – who were so destitute that they begged from beggars.

John Thomson/Hulton Archive

Diving into the Thames 1934

On a hot day in May, two boys launch themselves into the Thames within sight of the Houses of Parliament. The ornate cast-iron lamp-posts with their globe lantern and encircling sea creature – opinions vary whether it's a sturgeon or a dolphin – were erected in the 1870s, the finishing touch to the fine example of Victorian engineering and enterprise that is the Albert Embankment. It was built, along with Chelsea and Victoria Embankments, by Sir Joseph Bazalgette, also the mastermind behind the capital's sewage system. Lambeth Bridge (visible in the distance) had been completed a couple of years before, replacing a Victorian suspension bridge that had rusted beyond repair.

HF Davis/Hulton Archive

Rolls-Royce at the Hilton 1965

A doorman salutes as a Roller pulls up outside the Hilton hotel on Park Lane – it's the perfect image of urban glamour and sophistication in 1960s London. It was shot by Terry Fincher, one of Britain's great press photographers during Fleet Street's heyday. He started his 50-year career in 1945 as a messenger boy for the Keystone Press Agency, later working for the *Daily Express* and the *Evening Standard*, snapping everyone from Churchill to Mother Teresa to Great Train Robber Charlie Wilson (whom he'd known growing up in south London) and covering such landmark events as the Suez Crisis, the Vietnam War and the Biafra famine.

Terry Fincher/Express/Hulton Archive

Turtles for the Lord Mayor 1938

It's early November 1938, and weeks of preparations for the annual Lord Mayor's Banquet at the Guildhall (where it has been held since 1501) are nearly complete. The cooks, 36 in total, have amassed their ingredients for the gargantuan feast, which includes the traditional dishes of barons of beef, game pie, roast potatoes, orange jelly – and turtle soup. The total cost of the event, including food, wine and wages for the numerous staff, was £500. Thankfully, turtles are no longer required, but the banquet is still a major event on London's official social calendar. The guest list numbers in the hundreds, featuring cabinet ministers, Commonwealth and foreign dignitaries, and leaders from business, the judiciary, the church and the armed services; the keynote address is given by the prime minister. It takes place on the Monday following the tourist spectacular that is the Lord Mayor's Show.

Felix Man/Hulton Archive

Air-raid at Bounds Green tube
1940

Underground stations were commonly used as air-raid shelters during the Blitz – though they weren't a guaranteed place of safety. Two days after this picture was taken, a lone German bomber destroyed houses nearby, causing one of the tunnels to collapse and killing 17 and injuring 20 others – all of whom had taken refuge in the station. Bounds Green tube was only eight years old at the time, one of the new wave of modernist tube stations on the Piccadilly line designed by London Transport's in-house architect Charles Holden (who was also responsible for the University of London's striking Senate House). The lovely art deco bronzed uplighters lining the escalators still exist.

M McNeill/Fox Photos/Hulton Archive

Jamaicans in Brixton 1952

The West Indians arriving in London in the 1950s were sometimes met with indifference, occasionally with kindness, but often with ignorance, discrimination and downright hostility. Adverts for rooms or jobs specified 'No coloureds' or 'Whites only', and racist graffiti was commonplace: KBW stands for 'Keep Britain White'. Accommodation was scarce (a problem exacerbated by the post-war housing shortage) and was crucial in determining where the new arrivals would settle. People tended to stick in their own island groups: Trinidadians congregated in Notting Hill, Dominicans and St Lucians around Paddington, Montserratians in Stoke Newington and Finsbury Park. And Jamaicans headed to Brixton and Stockwell, which already had a black population, a lively street market, a friendly local council and plenty of cheap Victorian property.

Express Newspapers/Hulton Archive

The Sex Pistols 1976

'The Filth and the Fury!' screamed the headline next to this photograph on the *Daily Mirror*'s front page the morning after the Sex Pistols had sworn live on television at *Today* interviewer Bill Grundy. The nation was outraged and the band (from left: Steve Jones, Johnny Rotten, Paul Cook, with Glen Matlock at the back, soon to be replaced by Sid Vicious) garnered massive publicity as a result, bringing punk into the mainstream. The following year, the Pistols released the single 'God Save the Queen' (banned from airplay by the BBC despite reaching number one) and their only studio album, *Never Mind the Bollocks, Here's the Sex Pistols*, securing them a place in rock – and British – history.
Keystone/Hulton Archive

Pedestrians in the City
1938

In bright sunlight, City gents stroll down Throgmorton Street, long-time home of the Stock Exchange until it moved to Paternoster Square in 2004. It's an unusual image to come from the photographic studio Chaloner Woods. Working from the 1940s to the '70s, the firm was better known for its fashion shoots for the likes of *Good Housekeeping*, *Vanity Fair* and Harrods to use in their magazines and advertising campaigns – including early pictures of Roger Moore in his modelling days.

Chaloner Woods/Hulton Archive

Lights on Oxford Street 1939

A stream of lights wiggle down Oxford Street in December 1939. But the patterns are not made by car headlights, they're from torches carried by pedestrians negotiating the blackout. Imposed by the government on 1 September – two days before war broke out – to make it difficult for enemy bombers to navigate, blackout regulations were severe and strictly enforced. Householders had to completely mask their windows, street lights were turned off and vehicle headlights covered; even the red glow from a cigarette was banned. Cars crashed in the darkness and pedestrian accidents soared as people fell off bridges or into ponds, so some restrictions were lifted: torches were permitted (though had to be pointed downwards and the beam dimmed with paper) and white lines were painted along the kerbs and centre of roads. The blackout became a dim-out in September 1944 and was finally lifted in April 1945.

Walter Bellamy/London Express/Hulton Archive

Donald Bradman and fans 1938

Gobsmacked schoolboys can't believe their eyes as their idol, Australian cricket captain Donald Bradman, strolls along the Strand during his team's 1938 tour of England. Universally acknowledged as the greatest batsman of all time, 'the Don' was the most prolific run-scorer in the history of the game, amassing 6,996 runs in 52 Test matches, a batting average of 99.94 – a record that no other cricketer has come close to achieving. It was to counter Bradman's might that England adopted its infamous 'Bodyline' tactics in the 1932/33 Test in Australia. His career total of 211 centuries included three made in the 1938 series, in which Australia retained the Ashes; the intervention of war meant that it was ten years before the two teams met again.

Keystone/Hulton Archive

Emmeline Pankhurst arrested 1914

The most renowned member of the British suffragette movement, Emmeline Pankhurst, is arrested following a protest outside Buckingham Palace. Founder of the militant Women's Social & Political Union – whose members embraced direct action such as chaining themselves to railings, smashing windows and hunger strikes, in contrast to the more peaceful 'suffragists' – the high-profile Pankhurst was arrested many times during the first decade of the 20th century. Following the outbreak of World War I (soon after this picture was taken), she redirected her energies to the war effort, urging women to take jobs so that men could go to war. The Representation of People Act in 1918 gave voting rights to women aged 30 and over; universal suffrage for all adults (aged 21 and above) didn't come until 1928, the year that Pankhurst died.

Jimmy Sime/Hulton Archive

Gasometer
at the Oval
1953

Fans take advantage of a high wall in front of the gasometer overlooking the Oval cricket ground to watch a match without stumping up for a seat. Originally a market garden, the Oval was created in 1845 as the home of Surrey Country Cricket Club, founded the same year; the land was – and still is – owned by the Duchy of Cornwall. The first Test match in the country was played here in 1880, between Australia and England; two years later, Australia won the Ashes, leading to the famous mock obituary for English cricket in the *Sporting Times* and the cricket world's longest and most celebrated rivalry. The gasometer, familar to fans across the world, is now threatened with demolition.

**Edward G Malindine/Topical Press Agency/
Hulton Archive**

Weighing a penguin
1952

London Zoo's baby king penguin, Prince, is weighed by his keeper; at 13 weeks old, he tips the scales at 28lb and is, apparently, in excellent health. The zoo's penguins have always been favourites with visitors, though they've had a lot of competition over the years. Famous residents have included Guy the gorilla, Jumbo the elephant, polar bears Brumas and Pipaluk, giant pandas Chi Chi and Ming Ming, Goldie the golden eagle and American black bear Winnie (the inspiration for AA Milne's Pooh). The zoo has also housed some unnamed animals that have subsequently gained celebrity status through becoming extinct – such as the quagga and thylacine (aka Tasmanian tiger).
Fox Photos/Hulton Archive

Feeding deer in Richmond Park 1930

Motorists tentatively feed an intrepid member of the herds of deer, both fallow and red, for which Richmond Park is now famous. It was King Charles I who in 1637 fenced off the land for his personal use and introduced deer for hunting. Since then the landscape of the largest royal park in the capital has changed considerably as a result of the deer: pollarding was introduced to prevent them eating the trees, ponds were dugs so the animals could drink, and the ancient tracks and field boundaries became open grassland – perfect for grazing. There are also deer in Bushy and Greenwich Parks, but Richmond has the most, about 650, with numbers kept to a sustainable level by an annual cull.
Hulton Archive

Brunswick Centre 1973

The Brunswick Centre in Bloomsbury, a year after it opened. An early experiment in mixed-use architecture – the idea was to 'test' low-rise, high-density building, integrate housing and shops and provide a nucleus for future development – the project was the work of Leslie Martin (of Royal Festival Hall fame) and Patrick Hodgkinson for developer Marchmont Properties. Now Grade II listed, the residential and commercial complex got off to a distinctly inauspicious start when the developers failed to find enough buyers for the apartments and ended up leasing them to the under-funded borough of Camden for council housing. After three decades of neglect and having never really lived up to the initial hype, the centre was recently given a very successful makeover, emerging as 'The Brunswick' in 2006.

Peter King/Fox Photos/Hulton Archive

Anti-Vietnam protest 1968

London has hosted bigger and more violent demos since, but this protest against the Vietnam War outside the American Embassy in Grosvenor Square shocked the nation for its ferocity and strength of feeling – and for the number of casualties and arrests. On the morning of 17 March more than 10,000 protesters gathered at a rally in Trafalgar Square and marched peacefully to the square, where they were charged by mounted police after refusing to back away from heavily guarded barricades outside the embassy. Over 80 people were injured and more than 200 demonstrators were arrested. The event proved memorable for Mick Jagger, who was present; the Rolling Stones' hit 'Street Fighting Man' was directly inspired by it.

Potter/Hulton Archive

Children playing hopscotch 1950

Between its launch in 1938 and its demise in 1957, the ground-breaking weekly magazine *Picture Post* published the work of some of the world's greatest photojournalists, among them Bert Hardy, John Chillingworth, Felix Man, Haywood Magee, Thurston Hopkins and Grace Robertson. Bill Brandt also worked for the publication, covering topics as diverse as the latest evening wear, the bombed-out East End, National Trust properties, Hadrian's Wall – and street games. Hopping, leaping, vaulting, frog-jumping, swinging around lamp-posts, skipping, football, tig, rhymes and more were celebrated, alongside a plea for more car-free 'play streets' in which youngsters could play such games safely.

Bill Brandt/Hulton Archive

Covent Garden Market 1900, 1937

The bustling fruit and vegetable market in Covent Garden lasted for over 300 years, from the mid 17th century until it moved out to a new site at Nine Elms in 1974. In its heyday, circles of women shelling peas were a familiar sight in summer months. Their speed and dexterity amazed onlookers, but none more so than Mary, 'Queen of the Pea Shellers' – far left, in 1900 – who reigned supreme for more than 56 years. Up to 1,000 porters were employed to ferry goods around the market in wicker baskets balanced on their heads, and basket races were an annual feature for years; champion Jim Sainsbury was photographed (right, in 1937) practising for such an event with a tottering tower of 20 baskets.

Hulton Archive

AR Coster/Topical Press Agency/Hulton Archive

Rooftop anatomy class 1958

Taking advantage of clement weather, student nurses have an anatomy class on the roof of St James's Hospital in Balham. The general hospital (founded 1909) amalgamated with St George's in Tooting in 1980. As famous London hospitals go, St James's isn't high on the list, but it played a part in the Cold War on 11 September 1978 when Bulgarian defector and vocal Communist critic Georgi Markov died there, having been stabbed with an umbrella on Waterloo Bridge four days earlier. In an incident worthy of Ian Fleming, the autopsy at Wandsworth Public Mortuary revealed a tiny pellet had been injected into his thigh.

Reg Speller/Fox Photos/Hulton Archive

Cleaning Big Ben 1930

Mr Larkin, suspended by a rope more than 600 feet above the streets of Westminster, lowers himself down to clean a face of Big Ben, the clock atop the Palace of Westminster (though – pedants, take note – Big Ben is, properly, the nickname of the clocktower's main bell). The famously reliable timepiece started ticking in 1859; its huge faces, 23 feet in diameter, mean it is still the biggest chiming four-faced clock in the world. A Latin inscription at the base of each face reads: 'O Lord, keep safe our Queen Victoria the First.' And Mr Larkin too, one might hope.

Fox Photos/Hulton Archive

Flying fairies 1943

Despite their huge butterfly wings and beatific smiles, this group of Neverland fairies in a Christmas 1943 production of *Peter Pan* at the Cambridge Theatre would never have been as magical if they hadn't been able to soar convincingly above the stage. Thanks are due to West End master carpenter and technical wizard George Kirby, who patented the first theatrical flying machine in 1898. Kirby's connection with *Peter Pan* was long; he provided the flying equipment for the original production of the play, on 27 December 1904, with JM Barrie himself testing the harness in rehearsals. Kirby's Flying Ballets is still a specialist in aerobatics equipment, although, after four generations of Kirbys, it's no longer a family-run concern.

Kurt Hutton/Hulton Archive

Hitchcock in the Thames 1971

The murdered body of the Master of Suspense floats down the Thames after a mysterious assailant struck in the middle of... not really. In fact, this is a dummy of film director Alfred Hitchcock, used during the shooting of *Frenzy*, his penultimate movie and the first he'd shot in London for 20 years. The film opens with a sweeping shot of the river – but without Hitchcock's body (though he made his usual cameo appearance, wearing a bowler hat in an early crowd scene) – and much of the location filming took place around Covent Garden Market, where Hitchcock had grown up (his father was a greengrocer). Notable for some violent scenes depicting the 'Necktie Murderer', a serial killer who rapes and strangles several women, *Frenzy* is considered by many to be Hitchcock's last great film.

Popperfoto

Barbara Cartland
1930

Long before she became typecast as the
world's best-selling romantic novelist,
always wearing trademark pink and false
eyelashes, Barbara Cartland cut quite a
figure in London society. By 1930, she had
already worked as a gossip columnist for
the *Daily Express*, published novels, written
plays, married her first husband and hosted
an array of daring parties and theatrical
pageants, for which she often designed the
costumes (always interested in fashion, she
was an early client of royal dressmaker
Norman Hartnell). Here, she is in an outfit
representing Good Luck – note the horseshoe
headdress and stuffed toy black cat – for the
'Pageant of the Superstitions', held at the
Haymarket Theatre.

Sasha/Hulton Archive

Broadcasting House 1932

Costing £500,000, clad in Portland stone and containing 22 studios and a mile of corridors, the brand-new headquarters of the BBC opened at Langham Place the year this picture was taken. The asymmetrical, stepped-back design, by in-house architect G Val Myer, was to allow light into adjacent residential properties. Above the front entrance is Eric Gill's carving of Prospero and Ariel from *The Tempest*. Ariel, as Shakespeare's invisible spirit of the air, was chosen to personify broadcasting. Beeb legend claims that the sculpture caused controversy due to the size of the sprite's genitals, and John Reith, founding father and director-general of the BBC, ordered Gill to amend the work.

Hulton Archive

Cleopatra's Needle 1878

The 186-ton, 69-foot red granite obelisk known as Cleopatra's Needle is one of a pair (the other is in New York's Central Park) first erected in around 1,500 BC at the temple at Heliopolis, Egypt. It was presented to the British in 1819 by the Turkish viceroy of Egypt in recognition of Nelson's victory at the Battle of the Nile in 1798, but it wasn't until 1877 that a scheme was devised to ship it to Britain. Transported on a special cigar-shaped pontoon (and nearly lost in storms in the Bay of Biscay), the monolith was met by cheering crowds in London. It was originally intended for a site outside the Houses of Parliament, but the ground was considered unsuitable and it was erected instead on Victoria Embankment, opposite Embankment Gardens. Buried beneath the needle, a time capsule from 1878 contains that day's newspapers, a set of coins, a razor, a box of pins, Bibles, *Bradshaw's Railway Guide*, and pictures of a dozen Victorian pin-up girls.

London Stereoscopic Company/Hulton Archive

Soho's Gargoyle Club 1950

Founded in 1925 by aristocratic bon viveur David Tennant, the rooftop Gargoyle Club – on the corner of Meard and Dean Streets – with its Matisse-inspired mirrored interiors, was a glamorous and decadent hangout for the capital's avant-garde before the war. Artists and actors, playwrights and poets, bohemians and beauties drank and partied there, among them Dylan Thomas, Tallulah Bankhead, Noël Coward, Bertrand Russell, Graham Greene and Soviet spies Philby, Burgess and Maclean. By the 1950s, it had lost its sparkle and become more of a seedy drinking den, frequented by Soho's bohos and vagabonds, though it still retained a louche appeal thanks to the likes of Francis Bacon and assorted hangers-on.

Thurston Hopkins/Hulton Archive

Underground train 1900

This double-fronted tube engine was one of the first trains used by the Central London Railway (later renamed the Central line), which was designed to link the capital's western suburbs to the City. Opened in 1900 and nicknamed the 'Two-penny Tube' for its universal fare of 2d, the original route ran from Shepherd's Bush to Bank; now it's the longest line in the network, covering 46 miles and serving 49 stations. It also contains two of the Undergound's celebrated 'ghost stations': British Museum, located between Holborn and Tottenham Court Road stations and closed in 1933; and Wood Lane, added for the 1908 Franco-British Exhibition and Olympics at White City and closed in 1947 – though the station building remained for decades, its name and Underground roundel still visible behind layers of peeling red paint.

Topical Press Agency/Hulton Archive

Sadler's Wells Ballet School 1931

The godmother of British ballet, Ninette de Valois, inspects dancers during a class at the Sadler's Wells Ballet School. Although never a great star of the stage herself, she was nevertheless the biggest influence on the artform in Britain in the 20th century. As well as working as a renowned choreographer, she also founded the Royal Ballet, the Sadler's Wells Theatre Ballet (now the Birmingham Royal Ballet) and also the Royal Ballet School at Sadler's Wells. This picture was taken a month before a performance by the pupils of the school at the Old Vic – an event that is credited with heralding the beginning of professional classical ballet in England.

Sasha/Hulton Archive

Dog show in Hyde Park 1927

This picture was taken 30 years before the the spotty dog's popularity was boosted by the publication of Dodie Smith's children's classic *The Hundred and One Dalmatians* and the subsequent Disney animated film, but dalmatians obviously already had a place in the hearts of kids in London. This outdoor show may look rather makeshift, with the winning dog chosen, one suspects, simply because it's the biggest, but the dalmatian is a venerable breed, dating back as far as (possibly) Ancient Egypt. Named after the Croatian coastal region of Dalmatia (despite no evidence that it originated there), it has been used in multiple roles down the years – as guard dogs, hunting dogs, coach dogs and, in the US in particular, as firehouse dogs – but has probably lasted longest as the much-loved family pet.

Fox Photos/Hulton Archive

York Minster in Soho 1939

Not any old Soho pub, this: the tiny York Minster in Dean Street – once run by London's only French publican, Victor Berlemont, seen here mixing an absinthe – has always been central to Soho life. Famous during the war, when it was nicknamed 'the French' and was a meeting place for Free French troops, it was renamed the French House when Victor retired, and remains a celebrated and treasured hostelry. Mobiles are banned, there's no music, beer is served in half-pints (as it always has been) and the place still attracts an eccentric, boozy crowd of literary layabouts, artists, actors and general Soho bohos.

Felix Man/Picture Post/Hulton Archive

Jellied eels in Whitechapel 1927

Once an East End staple, jellied eels are no longer as widely available as they were in the 1920s. You can still find the dish in some of London's 20 or so remaining pie and mash shops, most of which are located in the traditional working-class heartlands of east London, plus a few across the river in Deptford and Peckham. And the Tubby Isaacs stall (established 1919) still stands outside the Aldgate Exchange pub in Petticoat Lane market. The main problem is changing tastes – although eel has resurfaced on restaurant menus in recent years, it's rarely in jellied form – but the mysterious disappearance of the European eel has also played a part. Stocks of the species have plummeted since the 1970s, and it's now classified as endangered.

Fox Photos/Hulton Archive

Oz Three 1971

The counter culture and the establishment clashed ferociously in 1971, in Britain's longest and most notorious obscenity trial. The editors of underground magazine *Oz* – from left, James Anderson, Felix Dennis and Richard Neville – were sentenced to prison for 'conspiring to corrupt public morals' with their 'School Kids' issue. The case garnered massive publicity, and involved a striking number of now-famous names: Deyan Sudjic and Charles Shaar Murray were among the teenagers who edited the offending magazine, John Mortimer and Geoffrey Robertson were defence lawyers, John Peel and George Melly were called as witnesses, and John Lennon and Yoko Ono helped organise protests against the trial. All three editors were acquitted on appeal.

Popperfoto

Festival of Britain 1951

Of all the structures built for the Festival of Britain, the slender, 300-foot high Skylon soaring gracefully above the flagship South Bank site was the best loved. Designed by Powell & Moya, it was nearing completion here. A contemporary joke said the tower was like Britain – without visible means of support. The aerial photograph shows other key festival buildings: north of the railway line and next to the Skylon, on the current site of Jubilee Gardens, is the Dome of Discovery (the largest aluminium building in the world at the time and packed with scientific displays). To the south is the Royal Festival Hall – the only building to become a permanent feature – and the chimney-like brick shot tower, built in 1826, which was demolished to make way for the Queen Elizabeth Hall.

William Vanderson/Fox Photos/Hulton Archive
Jimmy Sime/Central Press/Hulton Archive

Traffic at Elephant & Castle 1912

A typical road junction in Edwardian London: assorted trams, a couple of open-topped buses, a pair of horse-drawn wagons, a motor car – and a few pedestrians milling about. Horses were still a familar sight on streets until World War II and buses didn't get roofs until 1925. In fact, there's a complete lack of all the things modern road users take for granted. Although an early version of the traffic light (a semaphore system with red and green gas-powered lights) was installed near Parliament in 1868, it wasn't until the late 1920s that they became widespread. The first bus stops arrived in 1919, but people had to wait until the '30s for the introduction of road markings, pedestrian crossings, the driving test and the 30mph speed limit for urban areas.

Topical Press Agency

Diaghilev ballet 1924

In 1924, Sergei Diaghilev's avant-garde dance company the Ballets Russes appeared at the London Coliseum with a new ballet. With a storyline (created by Jean Cocteau) of bathing beauties and beach boys cavorting on the Riviera, *Le Train blue* was a heady mix of athletics, ballroom dance and Jazz Age modernity. It was also a triumph of artistic collaboration, featuring music by Darius Milhaud, choreography by Bronislava Nijinska (who also danced the part of the female tennis champion, second from right), sets by sculptor Henri Laurent, costumes by Coco Chanel and a front curtain by Pablo Picasso. The Ballets Russes' effect on the London lasted much longer than one production; among the many celebrated dancers and choreographers involved with the group were Ninette de Valois, founder of Sadler's Wells, and Marie Rambert, founder of Ballet Rambert.

Sasha/Hulton Archive

Jimi Hendrix at London Airport 1967

Looking every inch the epitome of a late 1960s rock band – check out the tasselled jacket and boots, the pyschedelic-patterned shirt, the cravats, the jewellery, the big hair, and try to imagine it all in vibrant full-on colour rather than black and white – here comes the Jimi Hendrix Experience. The main man is in the centre, of course, flanked by bass player Noel Redding (left) and drummer Mitch Mitchell. Three years later, after mesmerising appearances at the Woodstock and Isle of Wight music festivals, Hendrix died from inhaling his own vomit after a party in Notting Hill. He was 27. The counter-culture icon's former home at 25 Brook Street, W1 now carries the ultimate establishment accolade, a blue plaque.

Express/Hulton Archive

Raymond Revuebar 1960

The Raymond Revuebar on Berwick Street, with its red neon sign, was for decades a familiar feature of the Soho landscape. The first venue in Britain to host live striptease, the self-styled 'World Centre of Erotic Entertainment' opened in 1958. Paul Raymond, pictured backstage with some of his strippers, exploited a loophole in the obscenity laws by running it as a private club rather than a theatre. In 1961, a judge described the show as 'filthy, disgusting and beastly' – free publicity that boosted the club's takings. Raymond went on to become a billionaire porn magnate, publisher and property developer. A virtual recluse towards the end of his life, he died in 2008 at the age of 82.
Popperfoto

The Great Storm 1987

Not-so-well tended gardens in the suburb of Orpington, following the worst storm to hit Britain since 1703. On the night of Thursday/Friday 15/16 October, the south-east of England was battered by winds of over 80mph. The 'hurricane' left several hundred thousand people without power, caused the inevitable travel chaos (it was a question of 'trees' rather than just 'leaves' on the line) and flattened woodland across the region. It has also been suggested that the event contributed to the financial disaster of Black Monday – the first working day after that devastating weekend.

Popperfoto

Traffic jam on London Bridge 1900

Congestion on the capital's streets isn't a modern phenomenon – as this picture of London Bridge at rush hour, Victorian-style, shows. The 'new' London Bridge was constructed between 1824 and 1831 to replace the medieval original; by the end of the 19th century, it was a notorious bottleneck, having to cope with considerably more traffic than had been anticipated when it was designed (it was widened a few years after this picture was taken in an attempt to alleviate the problem). Now spanning Lake Havasu in Arizona, this is the bridge that was sold in 1968 to one Robert P McCulloch, who, according to urban legend, mistakenly thought he was buying the gothic glory of Tower Bridge.
Popperfoto

Sandcastles on Tower Beach 1955

The River Thames may be pretty clean these days, but the sight of sandcastles and paddling youngsters next to Tower Bridge is still a surreal sight. But it was once common. For almost 40 years, London had its very own artificial beach, created with tons of sand imported from Essex and piled up on the muddy foreshore on the north side of the river between St Katherine's Steps and Traitors' Gate. Aimed mainly at East Enders who couldn't afford a trip to the real seaside, Tower Beach opened on 23 July 1934; in the first five years, half a million Londoners picnicked and paddled, sunbathed and swam in the shadow of the Tower of London, or paid thruppence to hire a rowing boat to the bridge. The beach was open from July to September every year, with an attendant employed to look after the young. Although King George V declared the children of London should be given 'free access forever', the beach closed for good in 1971 because of worries about pollution.

Chris Ware/Keystone/Hulton Archive

Sweet rationing ends 1953

A mob of children rush a shop in North Acton on 5 February 1953, the day sweet rationing ended: it had been a long wait, over a decade. Toffee apples, liquorice and nougat were best-sellers, and some factories even gave out free sweets to celebrate the occasion. An earlier attempt at de-rationing sweets, in 1949, failed because demand far outstripped supply. Rationing was first imposed on 8 January 1940; essential and non-essential foods, clothing, furniture and petrol were all affected, though sweets and chocolate weren't rationed until two years later. De-rationing had a major impact on the confectionery market, with spending jumping by about £100m in the first year. Rationing of foodstuffs finally ended in July 1954, when meat was taken off the ration books.

Terry Fincher/Keystone/Hulton Archive

Peers at the coronation 1953

The eccentricity of the British nobility and government is displayed at its most delightfully bizarre here, as a group of peers hurry through the rain after the coronation ceremony of Queen Elizabeth II on 2 June 1953 at Westminster Abbey. It's a rare sight; the lords only wear their ceremonial robes and coronets in the presence of the sovereign, and these particular ones only for coronations. The designs date back at least 400 years (and the garments themselves can be almost as old, as they're handed down through the generations). The robes are made from crimson silk velvet, trimmed with white ermine, and the rows of black sealskin spots indicate the peer's rank; a duke has four rows, a marquess three-and-a-half, an earl three, a viscount two-and-a-half and a baron two.

Fox Photos/Hulton Archive

Chamberlain returns 1938

Prime Minister Neville Chamberlain returns from Germany on 30 September 1938, to Heston aerodrome in Hounslow, waving the Munich Agreement, which allowed Hitler to annex the Sudetenland area of Czechoslovakia. Although Chamberlain has been forever tarred by this extraordinarily over-optimistic moment, his policy of appeasement and the news that he brought back of 'peace in our time', as a result of his talks with Hitler, were greeted with jubilation. The rejoicing didn't last. Following Hitler's breaking of the terms of the agreement and his invasion of Poland, Britain declared war on Germany less than a year later.

Popperfoto

Euston Arch 1961

Euston Arch, the Doric gateway at the entrance to Euston station, was demolished five months after this picture was taken. Commissioned by the London & Birmingham Railway in 1837, the arch came to symbolise the towering engineering achievements of the railway network in the 19th century. Its demolition came, with what now seems like the inevitability of a Greek tragedy, when the decision was made to modernise and 'upgrade' the station following the electrification of the line. After much bureaucratic wrangling and several attempts to either protect or resite the arch, it was taken down and the rubble dumped in the River Lea in east London. There are, however, tentative plans to rebuild the arch as part of continuing redevelopment of the area.

Central Press/Hulton Archive

Jewish protest in Whitechapel 1919

The Jewish community of east London marches in protest against the massacre of Jews in Poland, a pogrom that was the result of the Polish-Soviet war and the fall-out from the Russian Revolution two years earlier. The Jewish population of the UK increased dramatically as a result of unrest throughout Europe in this period, rising from around 60,000 in 1880 to about 250,000 in 1919 – despite the designs of the Alien Immigration Act of 1905, which was passed specifically to curb Jewish immigration from Russia and Poland. Many settled in the East End, particularly in Whitechapel and Stepney, forming a self-contained world that had its own Yiddish theatre and newspapers, Hebrew booksellers, wig makers, ritual slaughterhouses and baths, Jewish-run restaurants and pubs, and the Great Synagogue on Brick Lane (now a mosque).

Topical Press Agency/Hulton Archive

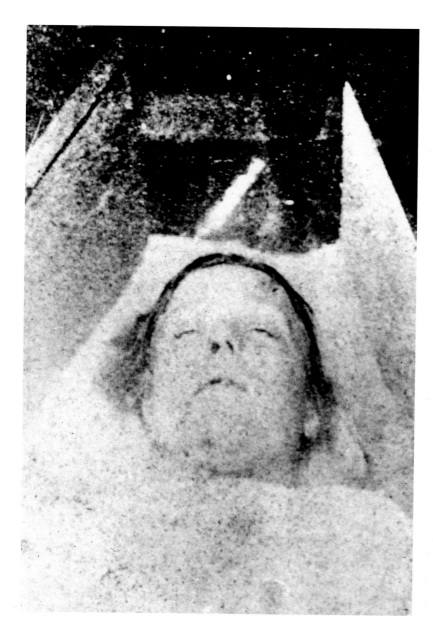

Jack the Ripper's first victim 1888

East End murderer Jack the Ripper still resonates as the first of the modern sex serial killers, and one of the few never caught. Of the five 'canonical' or generally accepted Ripper victims (there are 13 alleged others), 43-year-old Mary Ann 'Polly' Nichols, seen here in her mortuary photo, is thought to have been the first. Discovered disembowelled outside a warehouse in Buck's Row (renamed Durward Street shortly afterwards) on 31 August 1888, Mary Ann's story is a sad one, of alcoholism, family estrangement, years in and out of the workhouse and menial jobs, and finally threepenny prostitution – threepence being the price of a large glass of gin. She is buried at the City of London Cemetery in Forest Gate, as is fellow Ripper victim Catharine Eddowes.

Express Newspapers/Hulton Archive

Busking in Covent Garden 1952

In April 1952, *Picture Post* ran a story on Jack Irving, aka 'Charlie the Dancer', a busker who had plied his trade in central London for more than 40 years. Not one to be deterred by adverse weather, unreceptive audiences or the long arm of the law (he'd been up in front of Bow Street Magistrates 418 times by 1952), Irving performed song and dance routines for the queues of people waiting outside theatres and cinemas in the West End. Possibly Jack's finest hour came when Fred Astaire, on his way to appear at the Winter Garden on Drury Lane, commented of Irving's unscheduled performance outside the venue: 'I've got some people in the chorus in there who can't dance half as well as that.'

Haywood Magee/Picture Post/Hulton Archive

Notting Hill Carnival 1979

Held every August Bank Holiday weekend since 1965, the Notting Hill Carnival has grown to become the largest street festival in the world after Rio de Janeiro's extravaganza, attracting crowds of up to two million. Now a peaceful affair, in earlier years it gained a reputation for violent expressions of racial tension and frustration directed specifically at the police. The large local Caribbean community resented the police's increasingly heavy-handed attempts to maintain order – people were divided by barricades, sound systems were closed down early and crowds were forcibly dispersed as soon as night fell – and emotions boiled over in 1976, when a full-scale riot erupted. Three years later, as this photo shows, tensions were still high.

Evening Standard/Hulton Archive

Telephone boxes 1960

The red telephone box has been an instantly recognisable and much-loved symbol of London almost since its inception. The first kiosk, the mainly white KI, appeared in 1921, but it was the K2 – Sir Giles Gilbert Scott's winning design in the GPO's competition to find a new standard model – with its domed roof, multiple window panels and red livery that became such a familiar feature on Britain's streets. Modifications followed; it was the K6 of the 1930s that took the capital (and country) by storm; more than 70,000 were produced and the design lasted into the '60s. Many phone boxes were then sold off – as here, at the GPO's Dagenham depot, for a bargain-priced £60 plus VAT. Such was the worldwide appeal of the box that many ended up in the US and other faraway destinations.

Chris Ware/Keystone/Hulton Archive

Petticoat Lane Market 1962

Shoppers and stallholders jostle for space at Petticoat Lane in Spitalfields, one of London's oldest and most traditional markets. Sunday's the day to visit for bargain-priced clothing, bric-a-brac, cheap perfume, costume jewellery, household goods and general tat – gentrification hasn't yet hit this part of town. The market grew up around the garment trade that has long been a feature of the immigrant-rich area, from the Huguenot weavers of the 18th century to the Jewish rag merchants of the 19th and the Bangladeshi sweatshops of the 20th. Urban legend has it that the street was originally named after the silk petticoats on sale there, but prudish Victorians embarrassed by the mention of undergarments renamed it Middlesex Street.

Terry Fincher/Express/Hulton Archive

Index